BONETTI'S BLUES

Dundee Football Club
and its Cultural Experiment

BONETTI'S BLUES

Dundee FC and its Cultural Experiment

Jim Wilkie

MAINSTREAM
PUBLISHING
EDINBURGH AND LONDON

Author of *Across the Great Divide*

First published in Great Britain in 2001 by
MAINSTREAM PUBLISHING COMPANY (EDINBURGH) LTD
7 Albany Street
Edinburgh EH1 3UG

ISBN 1 84018 417 5

A catalogue record for this book is available from the British Library

Typeset in Berkeley Book and Transfer Gothic
Printed and bound in Great Britain by
Mackays of Chatham

CONTENTS

Introduction   7
Foreword   9
  1 An Unlikely Revolution   11
  2 The 1950s   21
  3 The 1960s   29
  4 The Late 1960s and 1970s   47
  5 The Late 1970s, 1980s and Beyond   57
  6 Do the Boardroom Shuffle   65
  7 Ron Dixon: Former Chairman   73
  8 Bob Hynd: Former Director, Board Adviser   79
  9 The New Era   85
 10 Season 2000–01   93
 11 So, Farwell then, Claudio . . .   109
 12 Jimmy Marr: Chairman   115
 13 Kenny Cameron: Youth Development Co-ordinator   121
 14 Season 2001–02 (Part One)   127
 15 Jimmy Connor: Director and Commercial Manager   133
 16 Season 2001–02 (Part Two)   139
 17 Season 2001-02 (Part Three)   143
 18 Bonetti's Scots   147

19 Season 2001–02 (Part Four)   157
20 The Fans   163
21 Ivano and Dario (Part One)   173
22 Ivano and Dario (Part Two)   183

INTRODUCTION

Blues – bittersweet song of life and love
Dark Blues – Dundee Football Club

Bonetti's Blues is for everyone interested in Dundee Football Club. It may be Ivano and Dario Bonetti who direct footballing operations and their exciting, new, cosmopolitan players who entertain the crowd but many others have helped create the right conditions for such an experiment, ex-players, administrators and – not least – the fans. I wanted this book to reflect not only this exhilarating (and occasionally frustrating) time in the club's history but also to remind people of some of the players who established the modern (i.e. post-war) tradition of good football at Dens Park. The key question in my mind was 'Why Dundee FC?'. For almost 20 years they hadn't even played lead guitar in their own city. Why did this imaginative leap of cultural faith happen here?

My thanks go to all the interviewees and, in particular, to Bob Hynd, Dave Forbes and Laura Hayes in the manager's office. Norrie Price's books *Up wi' the Bonnets* and *They Wore the Dark Blue* were invaluable sources of reference.

My love goes to Lorna, Eoghan, Jasmine and Dundee Gran, and I think it also appropriate to mention my favourite Chicago blues singer, the late Chester Burnett, aka 'Howlin' Wolf', who was born the year Dundee won the Scottish Cup.

FOREWORD

I first saw Dundee play (against United) in 1956 and I have watched them to a greater or lesser degree every season since. Having seen them win the League and play to a high standard in Europe, it goes without saying that the level of my commitment waned somewhat as I began to trudge to places like East Stirling (or Falkirk as it's known in the parallel world) in search of positive results and better football. Events of the last two seasons have brought me a whole new appreciation of the game and of the club. I wanted to record one story of how tradition, imagination and industry can maybe not *transform* people's lives but certainly brighten them through something as mundane or beautiful as a game of football.

I am, of course, talking for myself but another individual whose life was brightened by recent developments at Dundee Football Club was a big Dundee fan, Gerry McGrath, who died shortly before this book was published. I first met Gerry in the '60s when we were both teenagers in bands at the Top Ten Club and I will retain an admiration for his singing all my life. I was privileged to sing with the Dundee Mafia on a short tour in the early '80s and, when I subsequently wrote about them in the book *Blue Suede*

Brogans, Gerry chided me for mentioning his soulmates Doug Martin and Donnie Coutts, but not himself. It was a genuine oversight and I promised him, equally joking but serious, that he would definitely get a mention in the next book. I didn't know if there would even be a next book, never mind its subject matter.

The *Courier,* in a nice obituary, described him as a well-known singer on the Dundee pub music scene but Gerry was much more than this. He delighted punters in Dundee pubs and clubs for decades, but his powerful, high tenor voice (think Marvin Gaye) was of international quality and, when asked by the Average White Band star Hamish Stuart what his plans were, he apparently answered, 'Put it this way, I'm after your job.' His sense of humour was often disarming. I last saw him at Tynecastle when the Dundee fans gave a long, singing ovation to the Bonettis for what they had achieved at Dens in their first season. I'll remember that as a song for Gerry McGrath.

Ivano, Dario . . . Ivano, Dario . . .

Jim Wilkie,
November 2001

ONE

AN UNLIKELY REVOLUTION

'I've never played for a club like this before,' said Dundee FC defender Lee Maddison one day in the year 2000, and football aficionados knew exactly what he was talking about. A property magnate who thought he could buy and close down city rivals Dundee United when the latter were by far the more successful club in the town and their shareholding was in private hands; a lawyer who was subsequently struck off his professional register for financial malpractice and jailed; a Canadian wheeler-dealer who decided that an ice rink and a dog track held the keys to the city's footballing future – then two brothers who, whilst delivering major stadium improvements and success on the park, were briefly courted by the business associate of a notorious Serbian war criminal and driven to sack two managers who had achieved everything that had been asked of them. In the late twentieth and early twenty-first century, these were Dundee FC's chairmen.

Meanwhile, across the street . . . another chairman, a man who could legitimately claim to have done it all in football management, was torturing himself – and the club's fans – to death. Slowly and, in the manner of Torquemada, with absolute certainty of purpose.

In some ways, I blame myself . . .

When I wrote *Across the Great Divide* in 1984, I was an earnest laddie of 36, an innocent intrigued by the evident historic curiosities of professional football in Dundee. Why were there still two clubs in a moderately sized and economically challenged city? Why did they play across the street from one another? And why was sectarianism not a more prominent factor given the situation in other Scottish cities?

I laid out the facts as I found them in books and newspapers, tempering them with whatever insights had been gained over a 30-year period of playing football, watching the Dundee teams and listening to their exploits on the wireless. The publisher, one of whose fellow directors was Gordon Brown MP, had not dealt with football books previously and when he contrasted his failure to sell any books at the launch with his vanishing drink supply, he began to vent his spleen upon the author (myself). Naturally, he was consumed with remorse (and glee) the following week when special deliveries began to be requested by booksellers the length and breadth of the Murraygate.

His second football book, incidentally, was written by an even more complete literary novice called Alex Ferguson but, by then, the perceived need for intimidation as a publishing tactic had receded.

On the banks of the Tay, however, the pattern for weirdness was set in clay. A copy of *Across the Great Divide* – acclaimed by the *Guardian* and rubbished by the *Sporting Post* – had fallen into the hands of a diminutive millionaire named Angus Cook and, so much did he like what he saw, he decided to buy the company . . . or perhaps both companies.

Hermless

I don't know what type of person wants to write another football book. In fact, a few months before I began this, I was no longer certain that I wanted even to go to a match in Scotland. In my lifetime Dundee had plummeted from European semi-finals against AC Milan and Leeds to the B&Q Challenge Cup (which they won, but who exactly was B, not to mention his even more mysterious accomplice, Q?); from a League Cup win to League obscurity – and we're talking about the Scottish League here. The club's centenary video was celebrating goals against Airdrie. And all this against a backdrop of great United success.

In the millennium year, however, there was a new and unknown factor: an amazing decision by the new Dundee board to replace a manager – Jocky Scott, talented and loved ex-player with whom 90 per cent of the Dundee support were happy (although his teams were occasionally slow of foot) – with a new Italian regime. Not just an Italian manager you understand, but a player-manager, coach, fitness coach, club co-ordinator, later a goalkeeping coach and physiotherapist, plus a bevy of Italian, Spanish and Argentinian players. In some ways, given the relative size of the club, this was the most radical cultural experiment in the British game to date. Why? Why Dundee? Why must Jocky sleep with the fishes?

Then the first two games were won in marvellous and gifted style, so there I was at Easter Road, sitting a few seats away from middle-aged men I'd been at school with, hoping – 35 years on – for something. What? A glimpse of excellence? Some kind of artistic experience? Amazingly in one sense (but as was now expected), there actually was some art on show that day from Dundee's Caballero and Agathe of Hibs, and that doyen of sports commentators, Bob Crampsey, would remark later in the season that Dundee had reminded Scots that football could indeed be an art form. Were we trying to recapture our youth? Somehow reaffirm our identity?

The first time I went to the new Dens Park (in 1999) I went with my *West Highland Free Press* colleague Dave Scott, unwavering in his enthusiasm and now a DFC shareholder in spite of a fairly recent stroke. 'Is this your first time in the stadium?' asked a polite steward. Dave and I looked at one another, yon wye.

'No, we've been here before,' I said, 'but it is our first time in this new stand, and I have to pick up tickets.'

'Just round the corner then, sir, and your friend can hang on here.'

Changed days indeed, and greatly for the better.

I went round to the (temporary) ticket office and there was a wee guy in front of me, bending over to speak sideways through the space at the foot of the glass window. Acoustically speaking, this action was not really necessary.

''Scuse me, pal!' the man called, in a louder-than-necessary voice. 'Wid it be OK if eh bought a programme the day but didna go tae the match?'

The official paused for a moment, to consider this untypical request.

'Eh! . . . of coorse,' he said after a moment's hesitation, bringing forward a programme. 'Of coorse . . . one pound fifty, pal.'

'Ah, thank' very much, thank' very much,' said the wee man hurriedly. 'Y' see . . . eh'm a programme collector but . . . eh've got ti go tae a budgie show the day.'

> *Hermless . . . hermless*
> *There's never nae bather fae me*
> *Eh ging tae the libr'y, I tak oot a book*
> *And then I go hame for my tea*
>
> Michael Marra

Neither can it be obvious why so many people seem to want to write books about the Dundee although the transformation from juteopolis to 'international centre for life sciences and civic arts' must be one of the most remarkable events of my lifetime. Unfortunately it continues to happen against a background of poor life expectancy, but the city remains a vibrant place in my view and sometimes it's difficult to remember what it was, even in its relatively recent history.

Footballers can always be recalled, and incidents in the games too but, when you see pictures of the town in the post-war years, it really is another country. The famous photograph of United before their promotion-winning game against Berwick Rangers in 1960, for example – Ronnie Yeats, Denis Gillespie and the rest. These players will always be remembered as they were, but look at the crowd behind them: all men, most wearing caps, on an open terracing which was then still railway sleepers, and with free access for some determined young urchins through the smallholding fence. And why were there often smallholdings beside football grounds? There's one at Easter Road, too (although I believe it's under threat) and Hearts have a city farm near Tynecastle. Dundee also had its fairground – Gussie Park – in this area. Why? It's as though the whole place was some kind of no man's land available for community action and fertility rites.

Good sportsmen, I suppose, were always revered for the 'lift' they could give to the community – the 'I clapped his dug' syndrome – and Dundee certainly needed a good slap in the '50s. Jute was still selling but the bigger mills were beginning to close and, in any case, the factory lifestyle could not be sustained. People were having to work long hours in filthy, noisy conditions for subsistence money and even the clerical jobs harked back to another era. The Verdant Works in Dundee, now a splendid (albeit threatened) heritage centre, gives you an idea of what things were like – folk standing at desks, one telephone in the main office, hundreds of people queuing at the gate to run home (or to the pub) as soon as the bummer went. Any relief was welcome.

Another (related) feature of the city at this time, particularly in the streets which led from the docks to the mills, was horses. Carters apparently provided the most reliable transport up cobbled hills and the smell of the jute in the streets (not to mention the ordure) was memorable. In fact, in the '60s, there was a wee stables quite near the Dundee football grounds, in Malcolm Street. The clothing that these men worked in was also unique: bib and braces in better weather but, when it rained, on came the bunnets and long coats which, in time, were stained by the jute and the weather. In many Dundee pubs, this was the fashion in the '50s and '60s before the advent of the Pacamac.

Even sport had not really progressed from Victorian times in many ways. To get to the swimming baths you had to negotiate the wharves and another round of nightmare Dickensian employment opportunities. Many public parks – like Riverside – retained their original Victorian pavilions and sports changing-rooms.

So, post-war Dundee: trams; Ingin' Johnnies and singers in the back greens; the Overgate and Wellgate, curious and marvellous streets; the DPM (Dundee Pasteurised Milk), a minimalist café; Draffens, a genteel department store; La Scala, an ageing 'opera house'; Fintry, an avenue of hope; the Continental and Chalet, alternative dance venues with a whiff of extra-marital affairs; and Broughty Ferry itself, a holiday resort.

Into this scenario, in 1959, walked Bob Shankly. Actually, it might have been Bill Shankly who, apparently, also made a late application for the Dundee job – and what the legendary Bill might have achieved at Dens boggles the mind. Or does it? Could anyone have surpassed Bob Shankly's achievements at a provincial Scottish club?

At the time I was about 11 years old and going to Dens and Tannadice, week about. Dundee FC had, I suppose, become my team partly because my father favoured them and partly because they were the bigger, First Division side, but I always had a soft spot for United as well and, because the colours were quite similar, I wore the Dundee scarf to both grounds.

With rock'n'roll now awakening something inside me, I had noticed that not only could you hear Little Richard to best advantage at the Gussie Park carnivals (i.e. very loudly), but if you went to Tannadice early for some reason, you heard American country music that you didn't hear elsewhere – Hank Williams, Johnny Duncan and the like. There were also some memorable football experiences there: George Eastham playing like Maradona for Newcastle United in a friendly; Denis Gillespie and John White taking United apart in an Alloa team managed by Jerry Kerr; and the United characters themselves – Johnny Coyle, Jimmy Briggs, Walter Carlyle, Rolando Ugolini. Then there was the ground – the pavilion with one household bath and one phone where you waited for results at the end of the match; the wooden stand – 'every time the ba' hut the roof ye got covered wi' forky tailies!'; and the houses in the Sandeman Street estate that had an uninterrupted view of the United match.

By 1960, however, another factor had entered the equation: United won the first derby match since their promotion and were making clear their intentions to rival their neighbours on an ongoing basis. For my part, it meant that a choice had to be made and I decided upon the Dark Blues. The club appeared to have 'more' of a history, but I would pay for this.

In the late 1940s and early '50s, Dundee Football Club had ambitions to be the third force in Scottish football. Under the flamboyant management of George Anderson and chairmanship of James Gellatly, they retained the international outlook of wartime and brought a Scottish inside-forward named Bobby Flavell back from Bogota in Colombia, signed a Canadian, a Dane, various Englishmen and two South Africans and blended them with some young Scots talent like Doug Cowie, George Hill and Tommy Gallacher (son of Patsy and uncle of Kevin). Anderson then beat Rangers to sign the legendary Billy Steel from Derby for a UK record fee of £17,500 in 1950, thereby putting thousands on the home 'gates', and went on to win the League Cup twice (1951–52 and 1952–53) and reach a Scottish Cup final (1952). Steel only lasted a few seasons but was, in effect, the Claudio Caniggia of the side, enjoying great celebrity and the occasional commercial sponsorship. BILLY STEEL SAYS 'SMOKE CRAVEN A' was a cardboard sign that many Dundee children saw on the shop counter when they handed over their mum's ration book. There was also the occasional note of scandal with stories of the Scotland cap turning up still drunk on a Saturday morning, only to be put in a shower before going out to play a blinder. Changed days?

Dundee continued to attract young talent with Doug Cowie the vital link. A stylish footballer who was comfortable anywhere in the half-back line, he acted as mentor to the next generation which included Jim Chalmers, George O'Hara, Jimmy Gabriel and Bill Brown. The trend continued when Willie Thornton became manager and the ex-Ranger seemed to have a particularly good eye for young players. He signed Pat Liney, Alex Hamilton, Bobby Cox, Ian Ure, Andy Penman, Alan Cousin, Alan Gilzean and Hugh Robertson and, when he moved on – for family reasons, to Partick Thistle – the attraction of such a club to a man like Shankly who, himself, had made a good footballing reputation with a quality Third Lanark side, would have been fairly strong.

Shankly proceeded to take Dundee FC to their first (and only) League title (1961–62) and European Cup semi-final (1963) with a team which (again) Bob Crampsey has described as the most classical footballing side he ever saw in the Scottish club game. So that's why we were all at Easter Road. And it's why Hibs and Hearts retain a healthy support; why Aberdeen and Dundee United fans can never lose faith completely; and why Kilmarnock and Dunfermline fans soldier on in expectation. Because their football, at its best, represents their place, their art, their culture – in other words, themselves. Like first love, when you see beauty in the game of football in your home town, it somehow becomes part of you. You sort of belong to one another and the yearning appears to remain with you for the rest of your life.

Into every love affair, however, a little rain must fall.

'I found true love, weren't worth me waiting for . . .'
'True Love Blues' (Jimmy Reid)

TWO

THE 1950S

Doug Cowie

George Anderson . . . wanted you to get the ball
down and play football, and Dundee's always been
known for being a good footballing team.

En route to meeting Doug Cowie, I was imagining him as a fairly
elderly gentleman – and so he is, now 75 years old – but the fit and
lean physique which greets me on the doorstep takes me by
surprise and completely belies this age. What's more, it must be in
the genes, as he tells me that his son, Doug Jnr, is still occasionally
turning out for one of the Edinburgh Spartans teams, at the age of
50!

It may seem strange to begin this book with a player who was
born in the 1920s and then move on to three others – Alan Cousin,
Bobby Cox and Craig Brown – who plied their trade in the '60s.
What relevance can this possibly have to an international team of
highly paid players in the twenty-first century? Well, I'm sure the
fans don't need an explanation but, for the more casual reader, I
think it is important to understand something of the tradition of
Dundee FC: its players, administrators and fans, two of whom –
Peter and Jimmy Marr – have gone on to lead the club in this
exciting new era, risking substantial funds, built up over years of
business activity, in order to back a lifetime's ambition. Cowie was
the lynchpin of the 1950s side but, personally, I had read little of
his young life (or that of Cousin, Cox and Brown) and this is the
guiding principle of much of the book – asking certain individuals
to describe, in their own words, what they view as some of the key
moments in their lives, career and time at Dens Park. I also want
to know, of course, what they think of the current developments,
and to reflect upon what it all means for the quirky and unique city
of Dundee.

I view the '50s and '60s as the key time in the club's history and, as a result, have devoted relatively more space to players of that period than, say, those of the '80s and '90s. It was the time Dundee played their best football and won most trophies. A time when they were managed with flair and, because the teams of this era built up a large following, the club has been able to sustain a credible fanbase over a barren 30-year spell, hoping against hope that something interesting would happen again. Conversely, although the club had some excellent players in the '80s and '90s, their efforts were often overshadowed by boardroom developments which, accordingly, receive more attention later in the book.

For most Dundee fans of a certain generation (or three), Doug Cowie will be remembered as the quintessential Dens Park half-back – the club captain who led by example, an elegant passer of the ball who could also inject a little steel into the line when necessary and was good enough to play for his country, from a provincial club, in two World Cup finals. It is a classic Dundee football irony that Doug went on to spend as many years working with United as he spent with the Dark Blues, but such is football life in Juteopolis. Born in Aberdeen in 1926, he was the youngest of seven children.

'My family had always come from Aberdeen and, when I was young, we moved to the Torry district, south of the river. My father was a boxmaker and my three brothers all played Junior, all half-backs, and one played at East End with the goalkeeper Reuben Bennet, who later came to Dens.

'I went to Walker Road Primary, then Torry school and I always played football but by the age of 14 I was learning a trade in the shipyards – working with platers and riveters. We had a lot of good players just round about the doors and the father of one of the players – he was a fish merchant – gave us a full set of strips and the idea was that, if one of the local league teams had a spare Saturday, we would challenge them. Well, we had a lot of good boys and we would often thrash them. After one of these games – I was playing inside-right and scored two goals – Mr Walker, the fish merchant, introduced me to people from the Caledonian Juvenile team who wanted me to sign for them. He thought it would be good for me to play in an organised league every week.

'I watched senior football very seldom at that time. When you were very young, if your father was with you, you would be lifted over the turnstile but the only player I can remember making a real impression on me was Tommy Walker of Hearts. Funnily enough, I played against him years later when he came back to Hearts from Chelsea. Anyway, when I went to Caledonian, they played me at outside-left – and it was only when I played against one of my older brother's teams that Caley suggested I play at right-half against my brother (who was an inside-left). And I stayed there.

'Next I went to Aberdeen St Clements (Junior) and trained at Linksfield Stadium, near Pittodrie. My pal, Jimmy Paterson, also played for St Clements but he trained at Pittodrie. One day his father suggested that Davie Halliday, the Aberdeen manager, take a look at me, so then I went to train at Pittodrie and the next I heard, Halliday had offered St Clements a new ball. "You must be wanting something for this," said Mr Mackie, the St Clements secretary. He wanted us to play in a benefit match at Arbroath.

'So we headed south one Wednesday [September 1945] and I got to play the whole game. Jimmy only got the second half, however, and it was spoiled a bit by the older players not taking the match seriously. Before I could get my boots off, Davie Halliday says, "How would you like to sign for the Dons?" I said he would have to see my club secretary and he said he would see me the next night at training and asked me to promise I wouldn't do anything in the meantime.

'Well – I broke my promise and I don't think I've done so since. On the Thursday morning, I was moved from the shipyard to the repair yard, and somebody said I was wanted on the jetty. It was George Anderson, who had also spoken to me after the Arbroath match. He was sitting in a limousine and I was filthy but he insisted I sat in the back. Anderson had been manager at Dundee for about a year. He was originally from the north-east of England, had played in goal for Aberdeen and was apparently thinking about starting a Second Division Aberdeen team when he got the Dundee offer.

'Anyway, I sort of put him off. I said he'd have to speak to my father. He asked where my dad worked and, by chance, he was working nearby. So the old man came across, there was a bit of a confab, and eventually my father says "If you look after him, he can sign." You know this, from that day on George Anderson looked after me like a son. I started at right-half but Anderson brought St Clements to Dens Park as part of my deal and when the teams were read out, I was at left-half! It was a strange position for me but I scored and went on from there. People used to ask if I was left- or right-footed and that was good enough for me! I was actually right footed but my left was not too bad and it was at left-half that I eventually played for Scotland.

'This was more or less the start of the first really good post-war Dundee side. There was George Hill, Bobby Bowman, Ernie Ewen, Gerry Follon, Bert Julliussen and we won the Second Division. Then we almost won the First Division – if we had won at Falkirk on the last day we would have been champions but Alec Stott (unusually) missed a penalty and it just wasn't our day. Disappointing, but there's no point in making excuses. You cross the line and that's it. You must put your concentration into the game you're playing.

'The man who you might say was the tactician before me was Reggie Smith. He had been an English international from Millwall – which took some doing – but George Anderson had one good thing: he always wanted you to get the ball down and play football, and Dundee's always been known for being a good footballing team. The first time I came to Dens, I looked out onto the park from a long corridor. The grass was cut diagonally and Anderson says, "What do you think? If you can't play football on that, you'll never play."

'I was fortunate.'

Then, in 1950, Billy Steel arrived . . .

BONETTI'S BLUES

'He made a good impression in his first game and I would say that, although he was not a great trainer, at his best he was a world-class player. However, I also believe you have to be fit to carry your skill.

'We won two successive League Cups (1951 and 1952). In the first game, it was something to beat Rangers on their "home" ground of Hampden. We were down 1–0 at half-time, then 2–1 ahead when they equalised and took it to extra time. Folk always say that Rangers are the stronger side in extra time, but we scored just before the finish – Alfie Boyd. That was a marvellous time – the Scottish Cup final as well. But we were trounced.

'I first played for Scotland in 1953 and Steel was playing as well. Sammy Cox was injured, there were no substitutes and I went to left back, against Tom Finney who was a brilliant player – more profitable than Mathews because he could play anywhere in the forward line, score goals, lay on goals – but we got a draw with ten men: a "moral victory", and Archie MacAulay (Arsenal – later a Dundee coach) played in that game too. Gordon Smith was in the Scotland team around that time, George Young too, and I always liked Lawrie Reilly as a player, even when I played against him. He was always foraging and you had to concentrate for the full 90 minutes. But I find a vast difference with today's game. You could hammer in then, but there was nothing vicious – the tension in the game now, with tackles going over the top of the ball . . . although you could shoulder-charge in my day, and wingers would get bumped out of play. There was Bill Brown too – a great goalkeeper, very quick out of his goal and very agile. Although in some ways I had a better understanding with Johnny Lynch, the keeper before him. I would nod the ball back and Johnny would collect it. The first time I tried it with Bill, he was right behind me and the ball went in the net!

'Anyway, I went to the World Cup in Switzerland in 1954. We were unlucky against Austria, we might have had a point, but against Uruguay: 7–0! The Europeans always had better technique than us and we still haven't got it today. My last game for Scotland was against Paraguay in the 1958 World Cup in Sweden and Bill came in for the final game against France (1–2). He played brilliantly, but France had a great side at that time.

'When Thornton was manager at Dundee, I knew we had some great young players: Jimmy Gabriel – great, natural player, and most of those who went on to win the League – Cousin, Gilzean, Ure, Hamilton, Bobby Cox . . . I was lucky to get a game! It was slightly disappointing when I even lost my place in the squad, but I played for 18 seasons and I got to the top of the game. I don't think I was Bob Shankly's type of player and, since I was the last of the Anderson players, I think he was looking for a clean sweep.

'Then I went to Morton for a couple of seasons and I managed briefly at Raith Rovers. We finished in mid-table but there were one or two things I wasn't very happy with – players' contracts and so forth. So I went back to Hal Stewart and Morton as a coach and a couple of years later I got word from Jerry Kerr at United that he wanted someone for the reserve team. Fortunately we had kept the house on in Dundee and I was there for four or five years. I went out when Jim McLean arrived [at United], but he later called me back in as a scout and I had another 23 years! I also went to work at NCR [National Cash Register] when I came back to Dundee. I had my trade so I could work on the manufacturing side, and I enjoyed it. You could go home at night without the worries of football.

'I wasn't sure at first how Jim McLean would do. He was a tasty football player but I always felt he was a bit shy with the tackles. Then you would see the very hard language he would use on the players. The difference was like night and day! But he was a good coach and manager. He got things done and made them successful. Six international players in the first team and he was still hammering into them the need for success. Same with the reserves and youth team. He wasn't in the game to be in third place. He wanted to win at Celtic and Rangers, and Tannadice was like a fortress.

'At Dens they used to say we were a good football team but couldn't win anything. Well, currently they're a good team but they're no' winnin' either! So they should stop moanin' and get on with it. They're in Scotland now and they're not going to change the scheme of things. They have to get stuck in *and* use their skill, and then they'll be a good side.'

THREE

THE 1960S

This may seem rather obscure but I remember once reading an article by an Egyptian journalist who was in prison for his political views at the time that Mr Mubarak was installed as president. 'What was he wearing?' the journalist asked a friend, the point being that, if Mubarak wore a military uniform, the country was destined to witness a repeat of the mistakes made by some of his militaristic predecessors. Fortunately for Egypt, he was wearing a suit.

When I first heard that the Marr brothers were taking over at Dens, I didn't want to know what they were wearing. The first question I always wanted to ask when there was a change of ownership did not even concern how much money they had (that was the second or third question). No, the first question was, where did they come from? What was their footballing background?

When I heard that not only were they (or Peter, at least) of the same vintage as myself – which meant they had grown up watching the Shankly team – but that they also had gone through a footballing management apprenticeship in amateur and junior football, I instinctively felt that the club was going in the right direction.

As mentioned earlier, Bob Shankly was of the famous Ayrshire footballing family, brother of the Liverpool legend Bill, and he had managed Falkirk and Third Lanark before coming to Dens. His predecessor, Willie Thornton, had signed a number of outstanding young players but it was Shankly's ability to temper the side with a number of senior Scottish players which gave it legendary poise and balance. In his first season (1959–60) the club retained fourth position in the League but they slipped to tenth out of eighteen in 1960–61, one point behind United and ten behind third-place Third Lanark. Shankly obviously still believed in their potential, however, and having signed the veteran international Gordon Smith, was able to put a classic, free-flowing side on the park which would remain largely unchanged for the entire season and would win the 1961–2 Scottish League. The team comprised: Liney; Hamilton and Cox; Seith, Ure and Wishart; Smith, Penman, Cousin, Gilzean and Robertson. Additional squad players were Craig Brown, George McGeachie and Bobby Waddell.

For the 1962–3 League and European Cup campaign, Shankly brought in the former Falkirk and Liverpool goalkeeper Bert Slater plus some additional young players: George Ryden, Doug Houston, Alex Stuart and Tommy Mackle. The League campaign was disappointing (they came ninth) but the European games were unforgettable and they reached the semi-final: Cologne (8–1; 0–4); Sporting Club Lisbon (0–1; 4–1); Anderlecht (4–1; 2–1); AC Milan (1–5; 1–0). The Scottish international Ian Ure is just one of many players to have ventured that, with a kinder semi-final draw, they might have been the first British side to reach the final and even been the first Scottish winners of the trophy given the Wembley venue that year.

Alan Cousin
and the lapsus annorum or 'Meh, how time flehs'

Alan Cousin was not like other professional football players. When he broke into the Dundee first team in 1955 he was studying classics (Greek and Latin) at St Andrews University. I mean, it's hardly Gazza, is it? And at least one fan was heard to shout, 'See you, Cousin, the trouble wi' you is – a' your brens are in yer heid!' This did not stop him being an exciting forward player though – 'king of the double-shuffle' and fans' favourite before the arrival of the slightly younger Alan Gilzean, whom he still describes in wondrous tones: 'a natural goalscorer – ruthless when it came to scoring goals, he would push you out the road to score! He had an instinctive sharpness of just knowing where the ball was going to be and was such a gifted header of the ball.' The beauty of the partnership from the team's point of view was that while both threatened in the air, both could also score with their feet *and* distribute the ball.

Whereas Gilzean would come to represent the conventional goal-scoring, boyhood hero, Cousin, a modest man, in the 1950s echoed the Corinthian spirit of someone like Roger Bannister or Eric Liddell. In fact, as a student he actually trained on the West Sands at St Andrews – the scene which opens *Chariots of Fire* – and he still maintains that he really only wanted to be a teacher. Born and raised in the bustling post-war brewing and woollen town of Alloa (where he taught and still lives), he was good enough to be a county footballer at primary school but switched to the oval ball at rugby-playing Alloa Academy and was captain of the first XV (and cricket team), when a casual football game for Alloa YMCA led him to a spate of goals and national boys' club and youth caps. By then, he was also being sounded out by professional clubs and, destined for St Andrews University, had worked out that Dundee FC might be a useful sideline.

At this time there was no real sporting tradition in his family, although Alan's older brother Jim (who now runs Sauchie Juniors) also played senior football for Stenhousemuir and Stirling Albion. Music had its place in his father's exotically named jazz band – Johnny Cousin and his New Havanas. The most important thing for such a Scottish family at this time, however, was education. Like many of his generation, Alan's father had been a bright boy who had to leave school to earn money, so it was taken as read that, for Alan and his brothers, school was the thing and, although also a high achiever in the sciences, he opted for classics with French and sat a bursary exam for St Andrews.

Cousin explains: 'I didn't actually get the bursary and I think the fact that I was going to be playing professional football had something to do with it but, all in all, the university treated me very well over the piece and the French came in useful once when Dundee played in Lille in the Friendship Cup. We were staying in a small, northern town where no one in the hotel spoke English and Bob Shankly saw it as a good opportunity to make me work for my money: "Right Alan, come oan noo . . ." he said, "this is what we want . . ."'

As mentioned earlier, Cousin had actually been signed for Dundee by Shankly's predecessor. He recalls: 'Willie Thornton was a good PR man . . . very urbane, a good public speaker and someone my parents liked. I think I had been recommended to him by the former Rangers goalie Bobby Brown, who also taught in Alloa, because he was friendly with Thornton, and Davie Kinnear of Rangers had spoken to me previously. Anyway, by this time I had got a place at St Andrews and I signed a "post-dated" contract which allowed me to play in the youth internationals and go to university.

'The star player at this time was Doug Cowie. He was a great player, played with the side of the foot, didn't blooter the ball up the park and led by example. Tommy Gallacher was also a big help. I remember him taking me aside before we played St Mirren once and warning me about their big centre-half, Willie Telfer. Sure enough, the first time I go past him, he starts to threaten me. "Listen," I said, "Tommy Gallacher's told me all about you . . . " It was something you took in your stride.

'I signed in 1955. Cowie was the Scottish left-half and Bill Brown was soon to be capped and it was a big wrench when Doug had to leave the club. But then, it happens to everyone – the *lapsus annorum*. I broke into the first team in my first year and Cowie really set the tone at the club as far as playing style and tactics went. Don Revie was playing a deep-lying style and I tried this with the help of the senior players – coming back and laying the ball off.

'I created some difficulty for the club when I went back to university. They offered me training three nights a week at Tannadice (United were part-time then) but I didn't fancy that. I offered to train on my own, religiously, at St Andrews and Thornton's deputy Archie MacAulay drew up a programme for me. The only thing was, I wasn't privy to free-kicks, tactics and so forth, but I did the pre-season training and, after my wife and I were married, we took a flat in Dundee for the early season work.

'Also, from a money point of view, the bursary loss didn't matter so much as in my first year at university I was getting nine pounds all the year round, which meant I was quite well off. In fact, even when I went to full-time teaching I was earning more from football. However, it was never my intention to play football full time. I did my teacher training in Dundee and became a teacher – in Alloa as luck would have it, because a female classics teacher there had just gone to Canada. The football had just come along incidentally and this also caused some hiccups with Bob Shankly. But I had been training on my own for five years by then and he said he could live with my part-time football unless he thought my fitness was suffering, at which time I would have to go to train with Falkirk, three nights a week.

'With Bob Shankly, everything was different. He was much more "hands on", he wanted to know everything that was going on. Maybe he wasn't a great tactician but he knew the way he wanted individuals and the team to play and was not slow to tell players off: "What do you think you're doin? Get tighter on that man!"

'He also knew when he had a good team and didn't want to change it. A happy combination of circumstances meant that he had this group of good, young players and he also managed to get some experienced players like Bobby Wishart (who had been a good forward, yet went back to left-half), Bobby Seith, who had had great success with Burnley (English First Division champions) and, of course, Gordon Smith, who was used to success. We had been improving under Thornton but were not consistent and our professionalism improved when the likes of Gordon Smith arrived. Gordon watched his diet and you only had to look at him to know that it worked. He was 39 when he signed for Dundee and he was great with younger players. He'd tell them not to take sugar and he would drink hot water instead of coffee.

'I must tell you about one time after we won the League we went to New York. We were in a hotel when the American breakfast chef started telling us about the time he had spent in Scotland watching the famous Hibs team. We said, "That's Gordon Smith, sitting there."

"'No, no,' said the guy, "this was just after the war.'"

"'Well, that's him sitting there.'"

'Gordon looked after himself and encouraged others to do likewise – although sometimes it fell on deaf ears.

'I think we knew we had a special team when Gordon and Bobby arrived and Ian Ure suddenly blossomed as a centre-half. He was fanatical, he'd stay back in the afternoons, keeping the ball up – and remember, both our wing-halves were attacking players. There was no sweeper, so it was left to big Ian. He was also such a magnificent physical specimen.

'The other big influence was Andy Penman. He had been playing outside right but Sammy Kean [the trainer] knew Gordon from his days at Hibs, so when Gordon arrived, Andy moved inside. He was such a naturally intelligent footballer. Like Hammy, he could be as daft as a brush, but he was so good. Hammy was also neat with his feet and had bags of confidence when it came to taking players on. Bobby Cox was a better defender – he was as hard as nails, but a good footballer too. And Bobby Seith was a very clever player. He only got his English Champions' badge recently because of a bust-up with Bob Lord, the Burnley chairman. That was why he came to train with Dundee.

'We began to think we had a chance of winning the League; there was the Rangers match when we won 5–1 in the dark [it was foggy], we won 2–0 at Tynecastle, and then there was the incredible Raith Rovers match when we won 5–4. I also remember another game at Motherwell when we beat a very good team 4–2. But the Rangers match was terrific, really good. I remember the referee – was it wee Hugh Phillips? – respotting the ball after one of our goals. The Rangers players were always hard on each other, shouting and swearing, and Phillips says to me, "They cannae take it ye know, they cannae take it." That game was a landmark, although we had had a few good results against Rangers and they had such great players at the time – Baxter, McMillan, Millar and Wilson – that was what was so good about Dundee winning the League.

'We also loved Dundee as a city. These were glory days and there was the sheer excitement of going into Europe, although we never knew how things would work out and even in the first match, Cologne were one of the favourites.'

Alan Cousin was the forward famously involved in an aerial clash with the German goalkeeper in the first match at Dens.

'It was purely accidental. I have seen a photograph where it looks as though I was elbowing him in the face, but I wasn't even conscious of hitting him. I presume it was my elbow and when we landed he was out, with blood on his face. Mind you, we were ahead at the time [3–0] and we went on to score eight. But the return match was different. They had some great players like Schnellinger and we just could not get the ball. It was the first time this had ever happened to that Dundee team and when Bert [Slater] went off I think Andy Penman let in two goals and we lost 4–0. Then there was all the nonsense with the fans – they gathered on the touchline and one tripped Gordon Smith! Incredible. I do think, though, that our style of football suited the European game generally – playing the ball around, having options, route one if necessary.'

Bert Slater had come from Bill Shankly's Liverpool during the close season of 1962. Like Ronnie Smith of Celtic, he was a mature player who could bring out a fantastic or brave save that might turn a match.

'He could be absolutely inspired and in Belgium he had some wonderful saves. In Lisbon it was a case of battling and not losing and I always considered myself to be pretty fit, but you did so much chasing in these matches. And Shankly was aware of the need to hold the ball and not give it away. In Anderlecht, the headline was: DUNDEE, PARADOXICALLY, TRIUMPH 4–1.

'When we got to San Siro, it must have been terrific for the fans because at that time the European Cup was *the* competition and we were excited ourselves. We were reasonably confident that we could hold our own – and we hoped we might win! Although they scored early on, I equalised in the first half. Andy put over a great cross, the goalkeeper didn't come for it and I headed it down. We were quite happy at half-time but in the second half, the roof caved in. The big outside-left was towering over Hammy, and Bobby Cox wasn't playing so we didn't have our regular team. And the referee didn't help – he gave a lot of fouls against "Scottish" tackles. Milan had some great players though. I was in direct opposition to Maldini, who was captain of Italy.'

Cousin was the first British player to score at San Siro in the European Cup and when Paul Scholes scored there for Manchester United almost 40 years later, he was only the third.

'Ian [Ure] was the first to go [to Arsenal], then Gillie [to Spurs] but we were still a good side. When Bob Shankly left for Hibs, I remember Charlie Cooke had come and we beat Hearts 7–1. Charlie was shouting, "Give me a goal! I want a goal!" Well, Bobby Ancell made me his captain, with Bobby Seith as first-team coach but, eventually, I was out of the team and Shankly must have noticed because he then took me to Hibs and I played there as a kind of sweeper, behind John Madsen. Then it was on to Falkirk for a season.'

As Cousin's career came to an end he had a brief glimpse of what was to come in the Scottish and European game. At Falkirk, a senior player, Alex Ferguson, was beginning to establish some of his coaching ideas which, even then, says Cousin, showed imagination and freshness. Then, one day at Alloa Academy, Cousin took a telephone call.

'Hello,' said the voice, 'this is Jim McLean of Clyde. I've had a good offer from Dundee and I wanted to ask your opinion about a move to the east coast.'

'Go,' said Cousin. 'It's a great place. I'm quite sure you'll thoroughly enjoy it.'

Alan Cousin and his wife are now both retired from the teaching profession and, like everyone else, he watched Dundee FC's decline over the years with some despair. He is, however, enthusiastic about the current cosmopolitan crop. They also have a grown-up family to preoccupy them. Both sons, perhaps predictably, were good sportsmen – cricketers who played for Scotland at schoolboy level. And – also perhaps predictably – both have unusual and successful careers. One, Michael, is a senior lecturer in neuropharmacology at Edinburgh University. The other, Martin, is a concert pianist. It's *Johnny Cousin and the New Havanas* all over again.

Bobby Cox

Bobby Cox holds a unique position in Dundee's footballing history. Not only did he captain the League-winning side, he was born and raised within a few hundred yards of Dens Park and has continued to offer support to the club through thick and thin by undertaking a hospitality role before and after home matches and he still travels in the team bus as an ambassador. All of this was acknowledged when one of the new stands was named after him in the recent redevelopment.

Cox is a name which has strong associations with the town, principally through the Lochee mill of that name. Dundee had a wing-half in the '40s, Sammy Cox, who later played for Rangers. The Lochee branch of the clan has also supplied British theatre with one of its leading Shakespearian actors, Brian Cox.

Born in 1934, Bobby grew up virtually in the shadow of Dens Park, in Wedderburn Street. He attended St Peter and Paul's Primary School and St John's Secondary when it was located in Tay Square. His father and brothers were dockers but he was destined for a slightly different career.

'I actually served my time as a tailor, with Morton's at the top of Commercial Street and I was playing football for Osborne Juniors.

At school I was an inside-forward then a left-half with Osborne and I stayed there when I went into the army for National Service. I was in the Signals Regiment and based at Ripon in Yorkshire. Some English clubs were watching me there when a chap called Sandy Evans, who was a soldier with me and a provisional signing for Dundee, contacted the club and suggested they go for me before someone in England did. The left-back in the army team had broken his leg and I had moved back. I was engaged at the time, so it suited me to opt for Dundee and live in the town. I signed provisionally in 1955, then, finally, for Willie Thornton, in 1956. Alan Cousin came in around the same time and Bill Brown, Doug Cowie and Albert Henderson were the top players. Jimmy Gabriel came in after me – a class player, two-footed and a great passer of the ball. I also think Brown was the best keeper Dundee ever had.'

Two things stand out in my mind about Bobby Cox at this time. His terrific, outside-of-the-right-foot-sliding tackle (a Dundee pub was later named after it), and his jousts with the Raith Rovers winger Jimmy MacEwan. This led to a double sending-off in one match.

Bobby says: 'Jimmy was a pal of mine. We used to train together and socialise and go to junior matches. Folk would say there was a bit of needle when we played against each other – but it was nothing serious. He had far more of a dig at Andy Irvine who played left-back before me. He went to Aston Villa and stayed on in Birmingham. I've got his address on me right now in fact.

'Willie Thornton didn't impress me much – he was too canny to be a manager – and George Anderson was still there until the mid-'50s so Thornton was something of an office boy. Bob Shankly would not tolerate interference from directors and stopped them coming into the dressing-room. You knew where you stood with him – he had a good eye for a player and he didn't need to give us much in the way of tactics because he put players together who knew what they were doing. He would just say "go out and play" and we just felt we could beat anybody at that time, we were always going forward.

'In Europe, Real were the favourites and they went out in the first round. Cologne were said to be second favourites and we put them out. Milan was very frustrating for me. I had a cartilage injury but didn't know at the time and they took me over. I was gutted when I couldn't play. We had a couple of chances early on but the referee was very poor and probably cost us the game.

'I played on until 1969 – a one-club man. I played under Ancell and John Prentice, who showed some promise as a manager. I also thought Archie Knox would do well, but he didn't stay long. When I gave up the game I drifted away from Dens for a while and worked for British Railways. Then Angus Cook improved the facilities and I came back in the hospitality role.

'I like what is happening now, the team is playing well and there are some good European players – not all of them, mind you. But I think the Scottish boys will get a chance.'

Bobby Cox received one international honour, a League cap, but he was reserve to Rangers' captain Eric Caldow on a number of occasions and it was often said that he was a victim of Old Firm politics, a theory given more credence when the international position went next to Celtic's Jim Kennedy, then Davie Provan of Rangers etc, etc. Jimmy Johnstone recently nominated Bobby as the full-back that gave him most trouble in his playing career and ventured that he was someone Stein might have signed.

Craig Brown

I talked to Craig Brown on the day he announced what proved to be his last Scotland squad as manager. I felt slightly disloyal, as the foreigners who were giving the Dundee fans such delight might be seen by him as harming Scotland's chances by frustrating the development of local players.

In spite of aggressive obituary-speak by the journalists at the event, Craig rebutted such talk with an articulate exposition of the position as he saw it. At least one tabloid vulture who was ostensibly concerned about Craig's position – and that of the fans – was firmly reminded of his hypocrisy by the national manager, who still managed to retain his famous good humour throughout.

Craig was a squad and occasional first-team player in the classic Dundee side of the early '60s. When asked at the press conference why he had selected Gavin Rae for the Scotland squad, he replied, deadpan, 'Because he plays for Dundee . . .'

'I spent my teenage years in Hamilton,' he says, 'but, before that, I was in Troon in Ayrshire (my father was a PE teacher at Marr College) and I was born in Glasgow, in Corkerhill, the famous railway village [in 1940].

'My father then became PE Adviser in Lanarkshire and that took us to Hamilton, and he then moved to Jordanhill College to be Director of the Scottish School of PE. My father was a professional player with King's Park in Stirling and Partick Thistle, for a short time with Hamilton, and guested with Wolves during the war. The war curtailed his career but he was a big fellow, unlike me – a dirty big player.

'I was supposed to be a good schoolboy footballer. I was in the Scottish Youth team and Scottish Schoolboy team two years in a row. In the younger year (under 18s) I played with Billy McNeill and the next year with Alex Ferguson. Billy came from Bellshill and played for Our Lady's High in Motherwell. I was at Hamilton Academy and there was good, friendly rivalry.

'From there I went to Rangers at 17 and they farmed me out as a Junior, which I still think is a good idea. I went to Coltness United in Wishaw and Billy went to Blantyre Victoria. My father encouraged our football – we were three boys – but we also had to get the maximum at school and we all left with good Higher qualifications. I went originally to Strathclyde University to do a course in engineering but, after six months, I discovered two things: I wasn't really interested, and I was training at Rangers where the demands were great. So I changed course and went to Jordanhill to do PE from 1958–62. I was therefore a student when I came to Dundee in 1960.

'I didn't play for the Rangers first team – I played once against the British army in a low-key game but the reserves had some well-known players: Ian McColl, Sammy Baird and Johnny Hubbard, who had dropped out the first team. It was the time of Niven; Shearer, Caldow; Davis, McKinnon, Baxter; Henderson McMillan, Millar, Brand and Wilson. And when I went to Dundee, Doug Cowie was in the reserves there.

'I got an injury at Ibrox and wasn't treated very well because I wasn't very important. Originally it was a cartilage problem but I kept playing and it was swelling with every game and there was no physio. I went on loan to Dundee because Rangers wouldn't transfer me. Bob Shankly had previously tried to sign me for Third Lanark from school and remembered me. Now he only had 22 or 23 players and he needed cover at left-back for Bobby Cox.

'I was his first signing, a loan deal, in January 1960. I did OK, but I also went back to Rangers for a couple of games and played well, at left-back or left-half. So at the end of the season they wouldn't transfer me, but I loved it in Dundee – the Garvie digs, then Mrs Duncan in Saggar Street. That was Ure, Ryden, Tommy Mackle, Hugh Robertson and Doug Houston, who I recommended to Bob Shankly from Jordanhill. Doug was playing for Queen's Park and I said, "You'll get him for nothing." So that was OK by Shankly.

'I went back to Rangers but, in July, Dundee agreed a fee – was it £8,000? – and I was the first player he signed and the last he put away, to Falkirk, part-time in 1965. I taught in Dundee as a peripatetic PE teacher.

'Doug Cowie had been captain of the club and was now captain of the reserves and I played behind him. It was a joy. He would pull the ball down from shoulder height, he had wonderful control and great passing. And such a nice guy, although Shankly was phasing him out. If he was playing today, the sky would be the limit.

'The great Dundee team was almost complete. Gordon Smith was his best signing, although he was criticised for it. I don't remember tactics much, but he was a great disciplinarian. You had a job to do and he wanted things kept simple.

'There were no substitutes at that time, otherwise I'd have had a record number of substitute appearances! I was always number 12, along with Doug Houston, George McGeachie, Bobby Waddell and later Alex Stuart. We were the guys who went with the first team. Anyway, for the game in Lisbon against Sporting, Gordon Smith was tired at the end of the first half and Gilzean, who was a wind-up merchant, says, "I'll tell you what we'll do," winking to us. He used to call Gordon "the Gay" (as in "The Gay Gordon", Smith's honorary newspaper name, nothing to do with homosexuality) and says, "Right, the Gay, I'll put the ball inside the full-back and you run on and cross it. Anywhere in the box, I'll run on, head it in and make you a player."

'Gordon says, "Well, actually, Alan, I can't run . . . I'd rather the ball came to my feet."

'"Naw, naw," says Gilzean, "inside the back, use your pace . . ."

'Shankly the master tactician's phrase was, "Christ, Gillie, there's nae need tae get effin' complicatit . . ."

'A ball inside the full-back was "complicated" . . . Bob Shankly wanted it simple, very efficient and very fit. I once had a wee altercation with a parent in a Dundee school and got a black eye. So I told him: "Sorry, boss, this parent came in and did this."

'"Whit did you dae tae him, son?" he says.

'Bob was really concerned that football was a macho game and no team would overpower Dundee, physically. There was Cox and big Ure – and Bobby Seith was a powerful guy and Hammy had dig, so had Wishart. Penman supplied the passes, Gilzean and Cousin scored the goals. Cousin could put himself about and Gilzean was a dirty big bastard.

'It was also an intelligent side. I'd never seen anything like Cousin reading books with an apparent photographic memory, and big Ure was clever. He was good at crosswords so Doug, Tommy and I used to get the *Telegraph* at lunchtime and mug up on it. Ian meanwhile was at the bookie's and would come in later with five *Evening Telegraphs*. "Right – a competition," he'd say. Every night we would all finish one clue ahead of him and it took him three weeks to catch on.

'And there was Shankly's humour . . . The press would ask "What's the team?" And Bob would say, "Oor Greta hasnae picked it yet." (Greta was his wife.) Or else, "Same as the *Courier*."

'Alan Gilzean I remember very well. He only stayed in Coupar Angus but quite often stayed the night with us in Dundee. He was a terrific goalscorer – but not the hardest worker. You would come to the end of a game and his shorts would be immaculate. His balance was good but he didn't put himself about and scored a lot of goals towards the end of games when others were tired. He was wonderful in the air, a great shot. He came out one day for a pre-match warm-up. I can remember vividly, there was ice and he was playing in sandshoes, a reserve game . . . he was coming back from injury. This fan started to give him abuse. He ran off the pitch, jumped the wall and thumped him.

'I have great affection for Dundee. Much of the next period was disappointing and, of course, they let Jim McLean go to Tannadice. Jim was also thought to be a bit of a lazy player and, when he played for Hamilton, the shout one day was, "Ho, Accies . . . if McLean moves, follae' im. It's bound tae be half-time!" Yes, Jim was – shall we say – a rather "shy" and quite a lazy player whose success was built on demanding that his players were brave and hard-working.'

Of the recent changes, he says: 'I had not heard of the Bonettis and haven't met them yet, although I've been up to Dens once or twice to see Gavin [Rae] and it's a delight to see my old friends. I actually prefer to see players away from home when I'm assessing them, to see how they compete.

'People say Dundee are currently the most attractive team to watch and I don't dispute it. Now Gavin Rae, for example, is in amongst them and benefiting from the experience. And if you look, for the most part, at their off-field behaviour – their etiquette, their diet, their nutrition and lifestyles are those of professional players. And, of course, Kenny Cameron is looking after the youth development programme. Kenny is superb with the youngsters, so it's inevitable that [local] players will come through.'

FOUR

THE LATE 1960S AND 1970S

This, then, was the swinging '60s and everything, so far, was going to plan. The city of Dundee was making its name, once again, in Europe; the embryonic Average White Band (Vikings influenced by Poor Souls) progressing from the Palais in South Tay Street to the Marquee in London; and the town was becoming more acquainted with the gown via the conversion of Queen's College to Dundee University. There was even a whiff of revolutionary politics in the air although, by the turn of the century, Dundee graduate George Robertson would be a leading establishment figure as General Secretary of NATO and Christopher Chope and Brian Wilson would have held respective ministerial positions with Margaret Thatcher and Tony Blair. And, of course, there was also the additional home-bred talent. George Simpson, en route from the Dundee Tech to the position of leading British industrialist as Chief Executive of GEC/Marconi (before a spectacular crash); and future Labour MPs Lewis Mooney and George Galloway – the latter was planning to lead the city council out of the destructive mire left by Tom Moore and J.L. Stewart, then take on the world. Trumpeter Jimmy Deuchar was effectively leading the outstanding Tubby Hayes Jazz Quintet in the wake of John McLevy's stint with Benny Goodman; and the athletes Liz McColgan and Daley Thompson were future world champions soon to be born to Lochee mothers.

The football, post-1962, was similarly interesting. Charlie Cooke, of course, was in a class of his own and I have still to hear a better description than Iain MacDonald's (an Aberdeen fan from North Uist): 'Cooke seemed to have the ability to beat a man in slow motion.' I also have good memories of Alec Bryce and Joe Gilroy from Clyde, Jim McLean, George McLean and even Alex Harley, possibly yet to be immortalised in a Quentin Tarantino film, *Last Transfer from Third Lanark*. A friend of mine was once at a party in Dundee and looking for the toilet. When he went to try a certain door, an elderly lady (later identified as Harley's mother) said, 'Ye cannae go in there, son, ma Alex's shaggin' . . .' Then there was the Ulster flyer, Billy Campbell, taken off in a game suffering from hypothermia. Ah, the good old days . . .

John Duncan

'Get it to Duncan . . . !'

Finding a team to replace 'the most classical Scottish club side' was never going to be easy and replacing Alan Gilzean – as Jim McLean was to discover – would be particularly difficult. Remarkably, the club almost succeeded in doing both, although it took them another ten years or so.

Bobby Ancell had the hardest task, coming in after Shankly, but he had played for a good Dundee side and had carried the philosophy to Motherwell where he built an excellent, ball-playing team around the likes of Ian St John, Pat Quinn, Willie Hunter and Bert McCann. He didn't manage to win anything but – indirectly – he helped secure the city's footballing future by bringing Jim McLean to the east coast and also helping set up a new crop of youngsters at Dundee FC who would challenge Celtic and Rangers in the early '70s, win a trophy and produce a number of individual stars.

Partly because of his subsequent service to the club, Jocky Scott is the name most often associated with this time but there were other serious talents such as Gordon Wallace, Jim Steele and Ian Philip, plus the 'man who would replace Gilzean' ('Gillie' was actually his nickname for a while), John Duncan.

This is where I claim my place in the annals of Dundee's footballing history. (You will frequently find that Dundonians have a 'Zelig' or 'Forrest Gump' attitude to history. Ask them one of the big questions like 'How did Einstein arrive at his Theory of Relativity?' and the answer will almost invariably begin with a tenuous, personal link: 'Well, eh kent a boy . . .', or 'During the war, meh uncle . . .', etc.) So it was with me and John Duncan. Actually, so it was with every Morgan Academy footballer during the early '60s because, at the very moment that Gilzean was banging goals in across Europe for Dundee with head and foot, so the tall inside-left of Clepington Primary, Morgan Academy and Butterburn Youth Club, was doing similar business on the playing fields of Tayside. It was as though everybody knew that Gilzean's successor was in the pipeline – apart from one misguided Morgan PE teacher who banned the forward from playing in a Scottish Schools Under-18 quarter-final because Duncan wanted a rest the previous Saturday morning before an important youth club game. 'That decision still upsets me when I think about it,' says Duncan, 35 years later.

It was my particular privilege to play outside-left or left-back for various Morgan teams, so I really saw John's natural goal-scoring ability at close quarters. Sometimes you were fearful of going to head a ball for goal – particularly at a set piece – because you knew that, any second, you were going to be clattered by the full force of Duncan's challenge, never mind that of the opposition. The other side of it, of course, was the knowledge that if you could play a pass or flight a reasonable ball into the box, you were almost certainly 'making' a goal.

Then there was his 'fan club' to contend with. Every week, the left touchline would be thronged with his family and friends and every time I got the ball, the cry appeared to go up – 'Get it to Duncan!' However, we knew why then, and we know why now.

John Duncan was the most focused schoolboy player I can remember. Not for him the fripperies of fashion, music or whatever. It was all football, and it is a measure of his single-minded approach that he seemed to understand the value of specialist play even at this age. So what if some thought there were (arguably) better ball players around (Ian MacGowan and Ronnie Hughes are contemporaries that come to my mind); midfield players who appeared to have more drive (Peter Becker, Ronnie Scott, Ian Brown, Grant Keir), or other obvious major talents (like Peter Lorimer or Frannie Munro)? John Duncan was to be found in the penalty box, physically strong, arms outstretched, coolly getting the balance right and making that little bit of space for himself which would give him time to score another goal.

John explains: 'My family was very keen on football – both my grandfather and my father played Junior and I was kicking a ball before I could walk. At Clepington it was Primary seven that you got into the school team but I would turn up when I was in Primary five. I didn't get picked, but if somebody didn't turn up on a cold winter's day, I would get in and maybe get a goal.

'I was always a goalscorer and Dundee was always my team. My grandfather lived nearby and, from the age of four or five I used to go to the Dundee "A" games with him. I can remember players like Sneddon and McGeachie. I also saw Gilzean in the reserve side before he made the first team.

'I never, ever believed that I wasn't going to be a professional footballer, although I had some doubts about being retained at the end of one season with Dundee. I had played in the first team but hadn't done so well after college and wondered whether I would get a full-time contract. I played in Dundee Under-15 Schoolboys and got through to the last 44 for Scotland. Then I was watched by Andy Irvine and signed schoolboy forms with Dundee when I was 16 or 17. I also went down to Leeds just before this [the early '60s] when Don Revie was in his first or second year as manager and they were still in the Second Division. Peter Lorimer was there and just getting into the first team. Anyway, I played a couple of trial games for Dundee when still at school and got a couple of goals. Bobby Ancell then signed me (Bobby Seith was the coach) but I went to Jordanhill College and stayed part-time. After my first year, however, I trained pre-season and got into the first team with players like George McLean and Jocky Scott – but I was often knackered after a full week at PE college and I drifted out of the first team again. Jocky was exceptionally fast when carrying the ball and George Stewart nicknamed me "Gillie." John Prentice had become manager and I was really proud to be part of the club and play in the first team. It was difficult to match the '60s team but when we were in Europe we had one phenomenal run when we beat Cologne [Duncan scored a thrilling hat-trick in a 4–2 victory] and AC Milan at Dens. Duncan Lambie, I remember, was outstanding in the home game against Milan [2–0; 2–3 aggregate].

'Jim McLean made a difference when he became coach. He was very enthusiastic and gave the team drive and purpose, although I don't know if the results were great. His training methods were different: we worked on passing, tempo and touch to improve technique and there was a lot of running and hard work. He would also give you stick if he thought you deserved it. I remember him complaining about me shooting instead of passing (not uncommon for me!) but I argued my case and another time he praised me when I personally thought I hadn't done so well. There was definitely a rapport and we all wanted him to stay because it was a well-run club at the coaching level at that time. McLean also encouraged others – like Gordon Wallace and Doug Houston – who were students of the game and when I became interested in the coaching side I was one of the youngest to go to Largs on an SFA course. I got my full badge when I was 23.

'My game was goalscoring. I seemed to be in the right place at the right time and had the three important attributes: I could score with both feet and the head too. Also, my temperament was good. Before Tommy Gemmell came to Dundee, however, we were a good team that had won nothing. He was a good player who turned us into a team of winners (he scored a great goal in the League Cup semi) and I can't really praise him highly enough at that time [Dundee won the League Cup in 1973].

'I didn't think of moving on for a number of years but football is a short life and there was no freedom of contract so eventually I rebelled. I was scoring a lot of goals – I got two in a League international – and we had won the League Cup. There were rumours that Jock Stein was showing interest in me going to Celtic, which caused a bit of trouble at Dens, and I decided to go back to teaching for a while. I suppose this made life difficult for Davie White as manager. Bill Nicholson then came in for me for Spurs but the move did not take place until Terry Neill had taken over as manager and the team was bottom of the League. They were a big club, though, with some outstanding players – Martin Chivers, Martin Peters, Mike England, Pat Jennings, Steve Perryman and so on – and, fortunately, I scored a couple of goals right away.

'Pat Jennings was phenomenal. Quick, brave, agile, with hands like velvet. You would shoot from close range and he wouldn't appear to even look at the ball, just collect it. The team didn't win anything but we finished eighth in '75–76 and I was top English First Division scorer, with 20 goals. I had good contracts in London, I got married to a Scottish girl [they have three daughters] and played there for four good years. I played against some good people too. I did well, for example, against Bobby Moore but Martin Buchan was always a problem for some reason and Liverpool, of course, were the great team – they had people like Keegan, Toshack and Hughes at this time. It was something of a mystery – what was their secret? Just all good players, I think.

'Keith Burkinshaw became manager at Spurs and brought in Ardiles and Villa, just before I left. Glen Hoddle was also starting to come through – a fantastic player. I suffered a bad back injury which kept me out for a year. I managed to come back but I wasn't happy when I was left out of the team (I was maybe a bit big for my boots after getting all these goals) and I decided to move. I really shouldn't have; they were a good club to play for [he played for them 1974–78].

'In England, all they wanted was goals. In Scotland they had wanted me to develop my game and I learned a lot from Gordon Wallace in this respect – how to move, where to move. I also made the national squad but not the team; there were a lot of good Scottish forwards at the time – Law had come back, Dalglish, Jordan and Macari – so it was a bit disappointing. Anyway, Tommy Docherty came in for me for Derby and I played there for three years and the family has been in Derbyshire, more or less, ever since.

'I could have gone back to Dundee as a player, and I believe there was some interest later on from United as a coach, but I decided to try management and Scunthorpe was the only job I could get. The bigger names, like Emlyn Hughes, got the bigger jobs.

'I moved the family and soon wished I hadn't, because I didn't last long. In fact, I was kicked out when the team was at the top of the League because the chairman was friendly with the former Leeds player Alan Clarke, but I had done well enough to get another club and moved to Hartlepool (I can pick them, eh?). I was only there ten weeks before moving to Chesterfield, first time around. They were a slightly bigger club with gates of around 5,000. We got promotion from the Fourth Division to the Third and then Ipswich came in for me. They were a good club but in the Second Division and I didn't quite get them back up. We were seventh or eighth three years out of three. I brought John Wark back and there were some good young players like Dalian Atkinson and Jason Dozell, and my approach was simply to encourage team effort and organisation, which was not so popular then. It was also different from my own style as a player. But management was hard going and I went back to teaching for a couple of years before returning to Chesterfield, this time for seven years.'

John went back to Chesterfield in 1993 and, once again, secured promotion from the new Division Three to Division Two, in 1995. He narrowly missed the playoffs in that league before taking the club, even more improbably, to an FA Cup semi-final in 1997. The cup run plus subsequent sale of star players was said to earn the Derbyshire minnows two million pounds.

He continues: 'The FA Cup run was the fairy tale. We made the semi against Middlesbrough and it was 0–0 at half-time. I said to the players, "Right, this is it", and we flew at them after the break and went up 2–0. Middlesbrough got one back with 20 minutes to go and then this amazing incident happened. The ball hit the bar and appeared to go over the line. The linesman gave a goal but Ellery [the referee] focused on an incident in the box where he appeared to think the defender had been fouled. Then he realised that it was the attacker who had been fouled but gave this crazy decision against him. I didn't know all the details until later, I just thought it was a goal, and subsequently I was introduced at a referees' conference as the manager who was on the receiving end of one of the worst decisions of all time. Middlesbrough went ahead in extra time and we then got a last-minute equaliser to force the replay, which we lost.

'I am currently working as a players' agent with the former Liverpool Chief Executive, Peter Robinson, a really great man who had been through all the success with Liverpool. He set up a company in Norway bringing in Scandinavian players and knew of my contacts with the League Managers' Association. It's a full-time job but I still do work with the Association and I broadcast with Radio 5 and Eurosport. I saw Dundee just before Christmas [2000] and was pleased with the skill on the ball and team movement. It was an entertaining game and I also thought that the club was superbly organised behind the scenes. I was treated with great respect by Peter Marr and everyone at the club. How long can they keep it going? As long as they can keep coming up with the type of signings they have already made.'

FIVE

THE LATE 1970S, 1980S
AND BEYOND

BONETTI'S BLUES

Until the mid-'70s, the club managed to hold its position as a leading Scottish provincial side. Bobby Ancell gave way to former Scotland manager John Prentice and, with Jim McLean as coach, a bright new era appeared to dawn. Prentice, however, became disaffected and departed for Canada. Instead of promoting from within, the board decided to continue to pursue bigger football names and Davie White, recently sacked by Rangers, got the job. In one sense it worked: Tommy Gemmell brought his winning habit from Celtic, and terrific players like Thomson Allan, Iain Phillip, Bobby Robinson, John Duncan, Gordon Wallace and Jocky Scott projected the club into Europe and to a League Cup win, in 1973. McLean's departure, however, was to prove crucial. As manager of Dundee United he took that club to the front rank in Europe, while Dundee were relegated from the first Premier League (in 1976) and never recovered, yo-yoing between divisions for the next two decades. Tommy Gemmell succeeded White as manager and was himself replaced by Donald McKay, a former United goalkeeper who did reasonably well at Dens, steadying the ship and taking them to another League Cup final. This foundation was then very securely built upon by Archie Knox and Jocky Scott, who made a number of outstanding signings – John Brown, Robert Connor, Jim Duffy, Keith Wright and Tommy Coyne – and took the team to the verge of European qualification. This also coincided with what was thought to be positive change in the boardroom, but much of new chairman Angus Cook's good work was undone by the bizarre appointment of the unknown Dave Smith as manager and even his popular replacement, Gordon Wallace, could not reverse the trend. With the transfer of Cook's shares to Canadian businessman Ron Dixon, things went from bad to worse.

Bobby Glennie

'Ivano Bonetti's team? I wish I'd been part of that.
The type of player he's brought would only have
benefited me.'

Bobby Glennie is something of a Dundee cult figure, not for the usual reasons of starring in winning teams – although he did captain one to a League Cup final in 1980. No, Bobby is well thought of because of his efforts in teams which were often badly put together, driving his teammates forward against the odds. Physically, he is a very imposing man who probably put the fear of God into opponents, but he is also a thoughtful and engaging character who might have done better in management than one brief stint at Forfar. He played for Dundee for 12 years and, but for injury late in his career, would have surpassed Doug Cowie's record number of appearances. Now in his forties, he still plays an occasional game of junior football.

'I was born in 1957 and my family came from Dundee (my mother grew up in Beechwood and my father in the Overgate). My grandfather as a young player had a chance to go to Spurs, but the war intervened. I went to St Mary's, Lochee Primary, then St John's and I always played, usually captaining the teams. Dave Narey was a year above me at school and others playing at that time were John Holt [Stobswell] and Davie Dodds [Logie]. The first time I saw Dundee playing was against Leeds in the Fairs Cup. My father was a Dundee supporter. From school, I went to Aberdeen, although I had been down to Liverpool four times. They wanted me to sign but there was only one other Scot at the time – Peter Cormack – and I would only get home once a year so, aged 14 or 15, I didn't fancy it. This was Shankly's time and I played in his five-a-side team every Friday. He would never finish training until his side was ahead. But it was great: football all the time, with not much running and, of course, they had a great team – Keegan, John Toshack, and Phil Thompson was a young player.

'I went to Aberdeen early in 1974. Jimmy Bonthrone was the manager and a gentleman, although he also had a wee nasty streak, and the players included Buchan, Strachan as a young player, Bobby Clark and Willie Young. Ally MacLeod came later as manager, then Billy McNeill and finally Alex Ferguson. I played a few times in the first team and latterly with folk like Willie Miller and Alex McLeish. Alex had just come as a young laddie when I was at Pittodrie, although Willie was a first-team regular. They were good lads and a great pairing. I came home to Dundee in 1978 when I was 20, and Tam Gemmell was manager. Jocky was still there. He was a good player. He liked his wee moan, but I always got on well with him and I still do. Gemmell was the first manager to make me captain.

'Donald McKay, in some ways, was too polite to be a manager. He would want to talk quietly when you really wanted him to open up, kick somebody's backside. Archie Knox, however, revamped the place as soon as he came in. The stadium was run down (there were antique gas fires in the dressing-room) and he commanded respect, sometimes physically. He would slate you, but switch off immediately afterwards and have a beer with you. And there were a number of good players. There was Ian Redford at first, then Cammy Fraser (Donald signed him); Eric Sinclair (the Wildebeest); Iain Ferguson and Ray Stephen. Archie and Jocky made good signings too – John Brown, Robert Connor, Stuart Rafferty and then Tommy Coyne and Keith Wright. And I always remember wee Jimmy Murphy as a great player.

'Angus Cook meant well for Dundee but Dave Smith was a poor choice as manager. He continued to live in England, only coming up for the games and we hardly saw him. If it hadn't been for John Blackley, I don't know what would've happened. It certainly would have been better if Gordon Wallace had come earlier. Smith also released me on the Friday and Gordon came in on the Monday. He told me that he would've kept me on. He understood about continuity. United had the same six or seven players at the heart of the team for years. I would get someone [as a partner in central defence] for half a season or a season.

'Charlie Nicholas was a great player in Scotland at this time. He had everything. He would skin you, then let you get up and do it again. But I was only ever sent off three times, I think. Once, I remember at Parkhead in a cup match, we had gone ahead and, just after half-time, Murdo MacLeod was coming into a tackle with his foot up. It was right outside the dugout and you always know when you're in trouble, the referee makes a big play of it. Was it Syme who ran round me in a half circle and said, "You're going off. Violent play." My shorts were torn by Murdo's tackle and I showed the ref the stud marks on my thigh. Did he think I had done it to myself? He was arrogant. And, of course, the crowd was baying. It happened to me at Ibrox as well.

'We had some good, steady defenders at Dens – Tosh McKinlay, and George McGeachie, you knew what you were getting from them every week. And Jim Duffy too. I played with him before he did his knee in. The strange thing was that he took a while to settle in, five or six games, and Archie was giving him pelters. Then he would shout at me: "Get Duffy oot o' there!" (he liked to play deep, like Willie Miller). Later, Duff would say, "What does he want?" and I'd tell him it was just Archie, and just to stick with it.

'I went to Raith for a season and a half then I managed Forfar, with Ian Fleming.

'As for the current set-up at Dens, Ivano Bonetti's team . . . I'll be honest with you – I wish I'd been part of that. I like the guy's approach. The calibre of players he's brought would only have benefited me. And the attitude to training too. He has the young lads looking after themselves. When we were there, it was "away ye go home". I'd enjoy going back in the afternoons with the young boys. Of course, Bonetti has his problems too. The young lad Zurab can really play but if you saw them against Livingston, the big coloured guy Andrews was just knocking everything away. Of course, even at Aberdeen, Willie Miller would tell me to hump it up the park if there was trouble and we could reorganise. That's what the national players were saying. Big Wilkie has the physique and touch to play that role but maybe he needs a spell away from Dundee to get himself sorted out.'

Ray Farningham
Under-21 Coach

Ivano often speaks about the players' mentality. Ninety minutes' concentration.

'I was born in 1961, grew up in Kirkton, and went to St Columba's Primary, then Lawside. My father had had senior trials (Burnley was one) and he ran a local team, Duncraig from the Under-11s. He was a big influence on my career and there were six or seven boys there who became tied in with Dundee or United, training Tuesday and Thursday nights. I went to United first of all. Doug Houston was the PE teacher at Grove Academy when I was playing at school and he invited me to train at the Kingsway Tech. Kenny Cameron used to take the older kids, I was coming up to S-form. Jim McLean was the manager, of course, and he was just starting to put his great sides together. During the holidays we would go to the ground and players like Andy Gray, Ray Stewart and Davie Narey were there.

'From Duncraig I went to Celtic Boys and Paul Sturrock helped out there. He was only around 19 at the time, and the team were under 15. Ralph Milne was there and he had fantastic potential. He could have been really big but seemed to have problems off the park. I played inside-right or midfield although I was originally a winger and McLean thought I didn't have the pace for the position. He said if I wanted to make it I would have to change my game. I had one year's professional play, though, and Walter Smith took the younger players. He was a very good coach.

'I then went around a number of clubs. I was at Forfar for seven years, first of all with Archie Knox, who was first class. I was very disillusioned when I was released by Dundee United but Archie put me in the first team right away and also got me a job with Ramsay Ladders. Three or four times when he was at Dundee, I was supposed to be going there but, financially, I was better off with the job and the part-time football. I eventually went to Motherwell, where Tommy MacLean was the manager. He was clever tactically but there's so much luck involved, especially when you're a young player. At least I was lucky with injury.

'Motherwell were successful when I was there in that they were in the middle of the Premier League but I left before they won the cup. I went first to Dunfermline, then Partick Thistle and finally joined Dundee around 1992–93. Jim Duffy was manager and I got on very well with him. He was just beginning but he had a lot of good young players and the team should have been more successful. They had Wieghorst, Vrto and the ones who had come through the youth set-up, like McCann, Hamilton and Anderson.

'The boardroom stuff definitely affected the club – but not the players so much as the manager. The Simon Stainrod position was still to be resolved too. In the League Cup final year (1995), I captained the side in the semi against Airdrie at MacDiarmid Park and I got man of the match. It was a massive game for me but somehow I then found myself on the bench at Tannadice the week before the final and, although we won, I didn't get on in the final until the last 20 minutes of the game, by which time it was 2–0. I was gutted because I definitely felt we could have won that match.

'It was disappointing to come to Dundee so late in my career. As I said, I was almost here earlier, but Motherwell came in with the money. However, I played right through until we won the First Division under Jocky, so I saw the Marrs coming in. We noticed changes right away. Small things, which are still absolutely fundamental, like new studs for boots. The club had been getting run down.

'I had done coaching certificates, really just for my own satisfaction, and Jim Duffy asked me to take the young lads. It just went on from there and I've now seen Gavin Rae, Jamie Langfield, Derek Soutar and even Lee Wilkie and Lee Mair come through.

'All the different managers have really let me get on with things myself – as long as they see young players coming through. Ivano normally plays 4–4–2 and the young kids play the same system. I was on holiday when Ivano arrived so I didn't meet him until later. I had got on well with Jocky and didn't know how I'd be received. To be fair, they have never interfered and the bonus is that we have practice games every week – with the first team playing against Under-21s and youths – and it's through these games that MacKay, Forbes and Boylan have come through. I had major concerns about this at first, but this year they have proved that the young boys can make it and that has to be the case throughout the whole structure. There's also been a big change in the last couple of years in the local area. Kids are impressed by foreign players, they see their better technique, and that starts from an early age. It's the way Scottish football has got to go. Kenny oversees the really young boys right through to 16, then Stevie Campbell and myself take them to Under-21.

'I don't see so much of the first team but I'm interested to hear what certain people (including my father) make of it. You hear that they are brilliant as an attacking side, but maybe fail to kill the game off when they are on top. It can be a problem but I feel they'll get that right: scoring, and then concentrating on not giving anything away. Ivano often speaks about the players' mentality and this is what he is talking about. Ninety minutes' concentration. Consistency.'

SIX

DO THE BOARDROOM SHUFFLE

Angus Cook
Former chairman

In 1982, Dundee FC determined to become a publicly limited company and it was hoped that £500,000 would be raised in a public share issue. In the event, only £115,000 was raised and full-time football was only retained by directors Gellatly, Thomson, Lyburn and Marshall increasing their personal guarantees. The club, however, continued to sign and retain some top-class players (Jim Duffy and Colin Hendry for example) and, even when Cammy Fraser and Iain Ferguson went to Rangers, the astute transfer dealings of Archie Knox and Jocky Scott brought useful replacements, including Robert Connor and John Brown, and the club pushed into the top six.

In 1985, Ian Gellatly became chairman of the Scottish League, but by December 1986, and with Jocky Scott installed as manager, it was known that Gellatly would be opposed as Dundee chairman at the forthcoming Dundee FC AGM, and he had decided to stand down. His family association with the club had spanned four decades and the accounts, at the time of his departure, were said to be in a healthy state. His stewardship overall, however, had come in for a great deal of criticism over the years as he presided over the slow decline of the club as a provincial force.

His main opponent was Andrew Marshall, but Gellatly was in fact replaced as chairman by Dundee businessman Graham Thomson, while managing – controversially – to hold on to a place on a new, three-man board. Thomson was a former general manager of Timex. 'In business,' he said, 'I have never known the meaning of the word failure.' He was about to learn.

Another major shareholder, a Dundee property developer named Angus Cook, said he saw this as a hollow victory for the new board and, in the 1987 close season, offered to put £150,000 into the DFC company. Cook was another businessman who maintained that he had always managed to overcome problems in corporate life but, at this stage, the board believed that the offer 'was not in the club's best interest'.

Cook's mind, however, was made up. As a boy he had lived in the shadow of Dens and Tannadice, in Fleming Gardens, but unlike James Bond author Ian Fleming, whose grandfather's wealth had benefacted the small estate, Angus was not born with a silver spoon in his mouth. His soccer skills earned a trial with Cardiff City and he served an apprenticeship as a cooper (barrel-maker), then a Gas Board salesman, before entering the jungle of property development, where he survived a bankruptcy before making his million.

By September 1987, and with Tommy Coyne and Keith Wright leading another revival on the park, Cook had taken effective control of Dundee FC by persuading Gellatly, Ian Bett and others to sell him their shares. This prompted the resignation of Graham Thomson as chairman (although he remained on the new board as a director with Gellatly and Maurice Speedie, under Cook's chairmanship) and he would leave at the next AGM, ending an association with the club that stretched over twenty years. He cited a 'matter of principle', maintaining that the club should not be in the control of one man. Throughout sport, though, this was in fact the current trend and nowhere would it be more evident in the future than Ibrox Park where, in 1988, a Scottish steel magnate and friend of Graeme Souness, David Murray, bought the shares of Lawrence Marlborough (for six million pounds) to assume control of Rangers. His tenure would transform the Light Blues into a massive commercial and footballing success.

Back at Dens, Angus Cook soon announced that he had completed his investigations into the finances of the club. Debt, he said, was greater than had been earlier anticipated and stood at around six hundred thousand pounds between loans, overdraft and sundry creditors. The club's assets, however, he believed to be worth £4 million pounds and there was no truth in the rumour that he planned to build housing on Dens Park. Indeed, he had paid three times the face value of the shares – £300,000 to shareholders and a bank guarantee of £380,000 – although none of this, he admitted, went directly to the club. He was, however, considering utilising 200,000 shares which were, at that point, unissued and he hoped that new board members would come forward to take them up. In the meantime, there would be no cash for players, but he would give the business respectability by strengthening the balance sheet. Jim Duffy was announced as a DFC coach (injury had appeared to shorten his playing career), while former player David Johnston and Alan Paul formed the new commercial team and the club immediately looked forward to a new £100,000 shirt sponsorship from Novaphone. There would also be new toilet and training facilities and supporters would gather into an association. There was 'a long, hard road ahead', said the *Courier* but the future looked 'brighter' and the improvement in facilities was a very positive achievement.

The versatile John Brown, however, who had now been three years at Dens, thought it time for a change and requested a transfer. In time-honoured fashion, after an eye-opening display as a central defender at Ibrox, he signed for Rangers. The £350,000, said Angus Cook, would go on new players. He also claimed to have turned down an offer for Dundee which would have given him '100 per cent profit'.

The '87–88 football season finished, but the managerial merry-go-round continued, firstly with Alex Smith being sacked, exactly one year after winning the Scottish Cup for St Mirren. Ian Porterfield then resigned as manager of Aberdeen and Smith was soon en route for Pitoddrie, where – much to the consternation of Dundee FC fans – he was joined by Jocky Scott and Drew Jarvie.

Angus Cook's choice to replace Scott, however, came as a far greater shock (or, perhaps, mystery). It was announced that the virtually unknown Dave Smith, the Dundee-born manager of Plymouth Argyle, would fill Scott's shoes. Smith, who played for East Craigie, had left the city 38 years previously and comparisons were quickly made with the Porterfield appointment at Aberdeen. To make matters worse, the new man sported a haircut reminiscent of a certain circus entertainer and 'Coco' became his unfortunate nickname among the fans.

He was given some respite, however, when an amazing scenario began to develop 'across the road'. Jim McLean had been reported to the SFA following one of the Aberdeen semi-final encounters in which he had rushed to complain to Willie Miller about his role in an incident involving Paul Hegarty. The scenes had not been pretty and the football world was shocked, not only by the severity of the sentence (a £6,700 fine and a three-year ban) but also by SFA president David Will's somewhat overstated justification: 'The incident was potentially the most serious to happen in European football since the Heysel Stadium – and I'm not exaggerating. It could have been disastrous for us all.'

(Eh?)

McLean temporarily resigned as United manager, and chairman George Fox thought of doing likewise. It looked as though calmer counsel might prevail but the SFA ratified the decision and, returning from a first-round European Cup-Winners' cup match in Malta, McLean was involved in a most unfortunate incident. When pursued by a BBC cameraman, he lost control and head-butted the man, which resulted in a court appearance. United finally won the tie against Floriana, but would go out in the next round to Dinamo Bucharest 2–1.

There was better news for the city when Liz Lynch (now McColgan) won a silver medal at the 1988 Seoul Olympics and Jim Duffy returned to the game, first as coach with Airdrie, then as manager of Falkirk. There was no respite for Dave Smith who, having seen the club lose Tosh McKinlay to Hearts and slide down to second-bottom of the Premier League, resigned after only 217 days in charge. His replacement was another surprise: Gordon Wallace. The United coach had played for both clubs and briefly managed Raith Rovers. He apparently wanted another shot at management and, perhaps anticipating no change at Tannadice, reversed his boss's earlier journey. One of his first duties was to (reluctantly) complete Tommy Coyne's transfer to Celtic for £500,000. It was good business for the club though, Coyne having signed from United for only £75,000 a couple of years earlier.

Angus Cook's tenure as Dundee chairman was characterised by better figures, but also by a flurry of wheeling and dealing. Sponsors Novaphone were regularly linked with buying the club; ex-commercial manager Dave Johnston was said to have been behind a £1.5 million bid; and under the new umbrella of the Discovery Group PLC, the club was looking for a Stock Exchange flotation and a £15 million ground redevelopment. It was also reported that talks were going on concerning either a merger between United and Dundee or a ground-sharing arrangement, but this was denied by the clubs. Cook also tried (unsuccessfully) to change Article 74 of the DFC constitution whereby 4,000 shares would be needed to become a board member. Unfortunately, the team was once again slipping down the League during this period, and was relegated in 1990.

Once more, outwith the Premier League, the nature of the business changed. Cook retained full-time football but, as his losses began to mount, his business activities appeared to become more erratic. Debts were thought to have reached £600,000, then £1.2 million as the team failed to gain promotion, and the Discovery Group, now attractively renamed 'Disgorge', had gone into liquidation with Dundee FC becoming the corporate property of the Cook family.

The final desperate throw of the dice came in 1991, when Cook announced to an incredulous football world that he would bid £4 million to take over Dundee United, with the new team to be known as Dundee City. It was then claimed by Bob Jamieson of Novaphone that United had offered *him* money to take over Dundee. United denied this but, with both Jim McLean and Angus Cook acknowledging that a one-team city was the way forward and with civic authorities, enterprise companies and the like offering help, it is both inconceivable, and in my view negligent, that the clubs did not make some kind of joint progress at this time.

Of course, both sets of supporters opposed amalgamation, but ground-sharing seems the very least that could have been achieved, and in a purpose-built stadium. Instead, we now have two upgraded, but very old grounds in poor locations, ultimately in competition with each other.

Naturally, things got worse. The takeover was abandoned and, although not directly related, United also began a long, slow period of decline. A shareholders' association was established to oppose Cook and he soon announced that he had disposed of his 82 per cent shareholding and had resigned from the board to be replaced by his solicitor, Andrew Drummond. Drummond was said to have taken a 29.9 per cent share, with the remaining 52.1 per cent going to two unnamed investment companies. The fans were sceptical, suspecting a 'front' for Angus Cook, and the situation was not helped when Drummond introduced his partner Robert Prentice – nephew of former manager, John Prentice – to the board.

In fact, far from being a front for Cook, Drummond was actually defrauding his former chairman and fellow shareholders by disguising the total number of shares purchased and thereby paying less money for the club than would have been necessary under City rules (if he had taken a 30 per cent stake he would have had to offer all shareholders the share price he paid Angus) and later profiting from the sale to Dixon. He would later be found out, however, on this and other fronts. First he was fined by Dundee Sheriff Court and the Solicitors' Disciplinary Panel, then he was struck off by the Law Society and in the year 2000 he was jailed for embezzling £84,000 from clients.

SEVEN

RON DIXON: FORMER CHAIRMAN

In January 1992, Drummond passed the reins of power to a Canadian millionaire, Ron Dixon, although the solicitor would hang on for a number of years as company secretary.

In many ways, Dundee Football Club was fortunate to attract the interest of entrepreneurs like Cook and Dixon. The former was a dynamic local man who appreciated the importance of good facilities to the club but suffered from both bad judgement (Dave Smith) and bad luck (Gordon Wallace) in his choice of managers (I think Wallace would have done better if he had come in first). Dixon was much more of an international operator, was no stranger to major deals and both chairmen obviously were prepared to push the boat out financially for Dundee Football Club.

Principally interested in ice hockey, Dixon had come to Dundee at the behest of a friend, Malcolm Reid, to try to buy the Dundee Ice Rink. Apparently on a whim, he decided to shift tack to the football club which appeared to have enough ground to incorporate a new ice rink and, in time, a Dens Park dog track. Unfortunately, although on balance he enjoyed more football success than Angus Cook, his business life – a tangled international web of companies and banking arrangements – meant that (a) he could not afford to spend much time in Dundee; and (b) Dundee Football Club started becoming a tangled web of companies and banking arrangements.

He started well. The former Rangers chairman David Holmes was appointed (from Falkirk) as vice-chairman and Holmes in turn brought the flamboyant Simon Stainrod with him, initially as a player. The team was driving for promotion in 1991–92 but manager Iain Munro was increasingly being sidelined and was replaced by the English forward with Jim Duffy as assistant, both off and on the field.

In the personnel department, it is difficult to know where to start. Holmes' other businesses ran into difficulty and he resigned with Malcom Reid taking over the role as Dixon's lieutenant.

Stainrod was both a top-class player and a good early example of a coach widening his horizons. At one point he had an excellent group of East European players – Adamczuk, Czachowski, Vrto and Ristic – and when the names of the Dane, Morten Wieghorst, and Scots Neil McCann, Jim Hamilton and Iain Anderson are added, it can be seen that the management, in theory, was pressing the right buttons in terms of shrewd transfer activity and imaginative team-building.

The central problem, however, was that almost every deal brought with it allegations of confusion at best, and corruption at worst. There was Adamczuk – who was signed at a good price from Eintracht Frankfurt, allegedly sold on to Italy at a much higher fee which was never paid (the subject of a FIFA wrangle before returning to Dens), then sold to Rangers; Vrto – who was signed from the Czech side Banik Ostrava and whose agent requested £80,000 in cash to be handed over at a London airport; Wieghorst – who was signed for £220,000 from Lyngby in Denmark and who received only £80,000 from the middlemen; and Gary McKeown, whose representatives only saw £10,000 of a £30,000 payment from Dundee. It's little wonder that the Inland Revenue and Fraud Squad were at the door; that Neil McCann went to Hearts for a fraction of his worth (in order to keep the club trading legally); or that Peter and Jimmy Marr bought a car park next to Dens (to pay the club's VAT bill) before widening their business interest in the club.

And what about poor old Lochore Welfare? Having famously accepted a set of tracksuits for Gary Paterson, the Fife Juniors were compelled to remind the Dark Blues that a benefit match or £500 was also part of the deal. Could they get satisfaction? Ya boy, sir, could they wheechie.

Given the developing Bosman situation and the rise of the agent, I suppose it is to be expected that clubs were compelled to wheel and deal a bit more, and frequently with unsavoury characters. What is most depressing about the Dixon era, however, is the malaise which seemed to affect the club from top to bottom in its dealings with people. Indeed, one early business fallout – the appointment and rapid dismissal of Derek Souter as a commercial manager – would haunt the club throughout the Dixon era, ineptitude allowing the case to drag on for years, with the till registering more money at regular intervals. In the end, part and parcel of the Marr purchase was an agreement to sort the case out, which they did, partly by giving Souter shares in the club. Unfortunately this partnership, too, soon went sour.

Derek Souter was not the only disaffected (or sacked) member of staff, however. Chief executives joined office administrators and general sales people in the dole queue, and disgruntled trade suppliers, headed by the architectural practice Hiddleston, Hynd and Feist, formed a long line. 'Candidates had not realised what they were taking on,' said Dixon once, in a phrase of no little understatement.

A new, smaller board of Reid, Bob Hynd and John Black, with Robert Paterson as managing director (Nigel Squire would also later join the fun) managed to bring some stability to the situation and, after two years, the overdraft was said to be under control but the impression of constant firefighting would not go away. Funds were continuously being arrested by other clubs, businesses and even ex-managers (Iain Munro for example). The dog track did materialise but with more sackings and at an ever-increasing cost and, by the time Jim Leighton was paid for, the club couldn't afford his wages.

There was also a much-publicised legal claim against sports journalist Jim Traynor, then of the *Herald* and Radio Scotland, who was accused of slandering the club and defaming its reputation (which would have been difficult). The claim was later abandoned with both sides meeting their own costs.

By mid-1993, the maverick Stainrod had transgressed once too often and Jim Duffy was lined up as his replacement, a move hastened by apparent United interest in the 'bald eagle'. Duffy's transfer dealings (and principally Billy Dodds' move to St Johnstone) were not widely acclaimed but, as far as the board was concerned, he was getting the sums right and (notwithstanding early relegation) he was also getting some things right on the park, taking the club to its first (League) Cup final in 15 years in 1995.

The situation, however, was now being further complicated by League reconstruction which would demand that in 1997 or '98 clubs upgrade their facilities if they wished to have SPL status. This meant either new stands at Dens (10,000 seats were obligatory) or some kind of accommodation with United, to which Jim McLean was, apparently, resistant.

By mid-'95, the authorities were closing in. Originally alerted by the club to investigate transfer dealings, the Inland Revenue decided that financial irregularities were much more widespread and the statutory books were taken by the Procurator Fiscal. Andrew Drummond's financial affairs were also coming under closer scrutiny and the company secretary was forced to resign. Even the fans' behaviour appeared to be worsening. A violent 'casual' was banned from Dundee matches for life and some crazy, extremist stuff at the League Cup final resulted in mounted police charges and snatch-squad activity in the streets around Hampden.

Dixon was now gripped by paranoia as well as everything else – at one point he was found to be stacking furniture against his front door and was so worried by newspaper leaks he suggested a surveillance sweep of the boardroom. He hoped that re-registration as a private company might be the answer but this was resisted by Angus Cook among other shareholders and, in spite of Wieghorst's lucrative transfer to Celtic (with Barry Smith coming the other way), by July 1996 the board was being warned that it might be trading insolvently, and there was real doubt about the club's ability to survive. Neil McCann was quickly transferred to Hearts while a new director, Harry Leadingham, offered a short-term financial 'fix', but the writing was now on the wall.

Jim Duffy moved to Hibs and was replaced by his assistant John

McCormack. The team failed to get promotion (in 1997) but by then the Marrs had emerged as potential buyers and Dixon left the club as he had found it, with creditors at the door. He died in a car accident in Mexico in 2001.

EIGHT

BOB HYND: FORMER DIRECTOR, BOARD ADVISER.

BONETTI'S BLUES

There was always so much going on at this
club that no one knew about.

One of the unsung heroes of this period is Bob Hynd, who runs an architectural practice in the city. At one point he was asked by a fellow director to hand over his holiday money to pay YTS wages at the club and, like the diehard fan he is, he complied.

He was raised in a farming (and footballing) family in Coupar Angus. His father was a founding Blairgowrie Junior who had senior trials with Celtic, Kilmarnock and Third Lanark. One of the things Bob has picked up on is the loyalty of rural Angus, Perthshire and Fife Dundee FC fans who, he believes, did not convert to United one generation on, as they did in the city.

Bob says: 'Initially I went to work for my father on the farm until one day, at 9 a.m. and in ten degrees of frost, I had been dressing tatties for two hours when a neighbour, Peter Murchie, passed us in his Porsche – so I gave up a promising career as a tattie howker and berry picker!'

Hynd actually trained as an architectural technician but has made his mark in property development and now employs architects. This led him to his first work with Dundee FC in 1976.

'I was a home and away fan for ten years – 1975–85 – and I continued to do work for the club, free of charge, until I joined the board in 1992. The only job we had to charge for was the hundreds and hundreds of hours spent on the dog track, ice rink and new stand which, of course, was a financial disaster for the club.

'I always wanted to join the board because I knew I could save the club money and, just like any supporter, walking through the front door and having access to information brought its own reward.

'I knew Ian Gellatly and he was a Dundee fanatic but what cash the individuals had (with the exception of Andrew Marshall) was not up for being spent. They decided on a share issue (in 1982) because at least one wealthy property developer had promised to invest, but then he didn't, so most of the money came from small investors like me – £250 – and that was a lot of money to me. The big problem was stadium upgrading following the Ibrox disaster.

'We had worked (as architects) with Angus Cook and he had hyped up what he could do with the club. It was a time of hope and he accumulated shares by paying over score. Angus then put in a hostile bid for United because he felt there was uncertainty about the legitimacy of their (private) share issue and Dundee District Council was interested in helping towards a new stadium. However, this came back at £20 million when MacDiarmid Park had cost £5 million and that was what killed Caird Park, which would have been the sensible way forward. And whereas Jim McLean recognised the sense in having one team, he would only go ahead if it was called Dundee United.

'Angus is a very clever man. And Ron Dixon was the same, although they are different characters. In property, he could think ahead and was very shrewd. He also pressured the football administrators and this led to more friction with Ian Gellatly, who was president of the Scottish League, although it never came to blows – unlike Angus's relationship with Andrew Drummond.

'Drummond was Angus's solicitor and right-hand man in the share dealings and when Angus was under pressure he did a deal with Drummond who knew how bad the situation was. Drummond had bought shares in the name of various companies which he had set up with his partner Robert Prentice and by disguising the extent of his shareholding he avoided paying Angus the appropriate amount, due under City rules.'

Drummond, who would later be struck off his professional register and jailed, had also appeared to set up a back-to-back deal with Ron Dixon, but as Bob Hynd says, 'There was always so much going on in this club that no one knew about'.

Dixon had come to buy the Dundee Ice Rink and literally drove past Dens Park, asked what was going on there, and took a spur-of-the-moment decision to buy the club.

'His drive was incredible,' says Hynd. 'He would put in long days when he was here, but would not wait for bureaucracy, such as planning permission. His huge financial success had been "telecheque", a US cheque-clearing system, and nobody could quantify his wealth. But it came at a price.

'Everyone who has taken over the club in the last 20 years has more or less done the same thing. It's a fresh face, a new beginning, fresh enthusiasm and the fans get behind them – they're always given a chance. One way in which the Marrs have been different is that they are involved in so many companies, and sponsorship has improved dramatically. We used to have a difficult job selling corporate entertainment – there'd be 30 or 40 people on match days. Now the Captain's Lounge costs £500 for a table for four and there's a waiting list. [By 2001, annual turnover will have risen from £600,000 to £4 million during the Marrs' tenure.] They are also very loyal to those who work for the club; there are events for the staff with raffle money going to charity and so forth.

'I was right behind Angus when he came to the club and I thought he was the right man because his predecessor had no charisma whatsoever. I also had a lot of time for Ian Gellatly, whose heart was definitely in the right place, but he was always in his father's shadow. So I suppose I've offered some continuity to the club. This year we've done [architectural] work for the new club shop: there's a proposed new media lounge, we've upgraded the Captain's Lounge, we've just applied for licences for all the lounges. So we can be helpful in that area and on the safety front, but Peter has his own ideas about most other things.

'Going back a few years, I was the only director who backed the Marrs when they took over. Others were unsure because they were going to lose money on the share price. I was going to lose around £10,000 but I had not bought the shares as an investment and I was the one who eventually did the deal on Dixon's behalf in

Glasgow – at 4 a.m. The existing board then had to resign, but I subsequently got a call from Peter inviting me not only onto the full board, but also to be a non-executive director. The current board is Peter, Jimmy, Jim Connor and Richie Robertson, who is Jimmy's solicitor. Connor is the only paid employee.

'The Marrs are very family- and community-orientated and I think they reap the benefits. The last accounts [1999–2000] were not great because there was redevelopment and refinancing required, but Robert Douglas's transfer helped the trading position and Jimmy and Peter, I believe, have been prepared to increase their investment where necessary.'

NINE

THE NEW ERA

Peter Marr
Chief Executive

Of course, the budget went oot the windie.

Born in Dundee in 1951, Peter Marr was the third of six children and the oldest boy. The family lived in Lochee initially but moved to the new housing estate of Fintry when he was three.

'My father was always interested in football and was always a Dundee supporter – he took us to Ibrox when Dundee won 5–1 and we were also at the 7–1 win against Hearts at Tynecastle. Originally my father had been a mill worker who went on to drive a baker's van then ran his own mobile shops. Fintry was just beginning to develop then and so he opened a grocer's shop there.'

Peter played football at his primary school (St Vincent's) and takes great delight in remembering that 'this was the time when they won the AC Little Cup three times in a row with Frank "Frannie" Munro (later with United, Wolves and Scotland) as the star player'.

Although lazy at school by his own admission, as a teenager he helped found Fintry Amateurs (who then became Juvenile and went on to challenge the leading Fairfield club). Peter then managed Timex Amateurs before assisting another amateur club, Tayport, into the Junior ranks (with Dave Baikie), then lifting Dundee's St Joseph's to the upper echelons of Scottish Junior football. Tayport went on to win the Scottish Junior Cup and St Joseph's were able to match (and, indeed, surpass) them in the local leagues. I would say that it is this interest in the mechanics of football clubs at all playing levels which prepared him for his rapid rise to the senior ranks of Scottish football.

There is also, of course, the small matter of his business acumen.

'About 20 years ago, my father's business had gone down and I had an opportunity to get involved with a mate, Davie Young, in a project at the then St James Social Club, which we converted into the Venue in Constable Street. There was a split-up at this point and I went into a grocery business in Park Avenue before taking on the Central Bar in Commercial Street and other pubs including the Mardi Gras nightclub with my brother, Jimmy. We then moved into nursing homes for the elderly and mentally handicapped and, finally, a construction company to build such places. This business was sold on quite successfully a few years ago. We always had this thing about working for ourselves.

'We were five years with St Joseph's so we must have started there around 1982. They were second bottom of the Second Division and won it the following year. We then went on to win the First Division and various cups. Even when Tayport were getting to the Scottish final we were beating them regularly and winning everything locally. Again, this was with Davie Young, after my time at Tayport. Tayport were a well-run club and we signed eight or ten of the best amateurs in the area but I was never going to get total control in the way that I like to have it, so I left Dave Baikie there and went to St Joseph's.

'Kenny Cameron was then headhunted from Dundee United where he ran the youth system. We needed somebody that was really dedicated and he was pally with Dave Young. He worked in sports management at the college in Old Glamis Road, and still does, although he now does a part-time youth job with Dundee too.

'In the light of our success, I had an idea for Dundee. I didn't want to invest any money – I just thought I had been successful running clubs and I though I could make a success of running Dundee. I met Ron Dixon in Seattle but he did not want what I was offering and what he was effectively saying was that if he did not find a buyer, he was going to shut the club down. We had good income coming from the Mardi Gras, so we went into negotiations with Dixon for his shares. This was not easy and we had a hard time trying to do a straightforward business deal. He was very difficult to pin down and had this international wheeler-dealer reputation, banking in Russia and the Philippines and so on. He had also lost interest in the club and said if this fell through, he would close the club, sell the players and sell the land.

'Anyway, we managed to do the deal in June 1997 in time for the new season but the place was very run down. Morale was low, there was one girl in the front office and the lounges were not being used, but John McCormack was the manager and he did a good job, bringing in some good players like Jim McInally and Brian Irvine, then James Grady and Robert Douglas. And Kenny Cameron came in to run the youth policy with Ray Farningham.

'John was a decent manager but, because of the SPL situation which I was heavily involved with, promotion was the number-one priority. He had taken us 12 points clear at one point but the lead began to slip and I thought we had to do something. Replacing him was not a difficult business decision, given our ambitions, but it was obviously difficult personally.

'When we came in, we thought we would give it five years. With the SPL changing their plans we had to get promotion immediately and then we only had one year to upgrade the stadium. We had sold the Mardi Gras and couldn't raise the money to build the stands. For the first time in my life, the banking people had said no. So we were going to have to battle.

'Jocky Scott was working month to month with United at the time. We looked at his record which showed him to be a decent coach and he wasn't going to demand a lot of money – which we didn't have anyway. We gave him a two-and-a-half-year contract in the hope that we would get promoted – which he achieved – and just planned to take it from there. In all the turmoil of the next year – the stands, Di Stefano (Italian agent, thought to be fronting a Serbian company who offered to put money into the club) and all this – he took us to fifth. Unbelievable. But still at the back of my mind was: one more year of his contract, and what then?

BONETTI'S BLUES

'About this time last year [winter 1999] Ivano Bonetti came across. I had met Dario Magri through a Yugoslavian agent and Dario came up with Patrizio Billio and Walter Del Rio. They played in an Under-21 match at Tannadice and Dario said that his cousin Ivano, who had been at Grimsby and Tranmere, might also like to play here. Ivano came over and we talked about him coming as a player. Unfortunately, Jocky wasn't too keen on foreign players so we left it but, later, Jim Connor came to me to say that Ivano and his older brother Dario were interested in management. They were involved with a Serie D team or something – Sestrese. Now, we knew Jocky and were happy with him but he had a problem with the players that Steve Archibald had introduced (including Luna and Artero) although he wasn't bringing in new players of his own, and the threat of relegation was still there.

'I went from Mallorca to Genoa and met Ivano and Dario. I gave them certain criteria which asked where they thought Dundee could go with them in charge; what connections they had to bring in players; what sort of budget would they need, and what the long-term goal was. I gave Jocky the same criteria and I also met Berndt Schuster at Barcelona via Steve Archibald asked him also.

'Ivano answered the questions over the weekend I was in Genoa and the thing I liked about him was that he played a wee trick on me. We were sitting in his back garden and I was waiting for an update from Dens where we were playing Hearts. He was typing information into his computer and asked me for my mobile number to type in. Ten minutes into the second half, the phone goes and a voice says: "Dundee: 1; Hearts: 0".

'"Who is this?" I ask.

'"Ha, ha!" says the voice, "it's me, Ivano!" I thought, brilliant, this man is a character. I met Schuster and he was a bit droll, like Jocky. Obviously, Schuster's CV matched Ivano and Dario's and Jocky was a good, solid coach but, when I looked at their connections, I thought – Ivano's the man.

'We battled hard on the contract and eventually he said, "I will join you on your adventure." I said "No, *I* will join you on *your* adventure."

'Jocky was messed about something terrible. We didn't have Ivano signed up at first and the number-one thing was to look after the club. If Ivano had said no, it would have been Jocky again, although I don't think it would have excited the fans in the way Ivano and Dario have excited the fans. I have got to say that the initial budget I gave them has gone oot the windie but the excitement, the backing we've had from the fans, the profile of the club . . . when you were abroad, it used to always be "Dundee United" and they deserved it – the wee man did a great job.

'We work at being a family club. We always try to treat everybody the same. The football side will always change but it's 100 per cent Dundee people here. It's early days. We're six months into it [Christmas 2000] and I have always said, wait till the second half of the season. It was a huge blow when we lost Caballero so early. He looked fantastic but, at the same time young Milne and Sara are working really hard now. I've not seen too much of the coaching but I know those guys work hard too, working with individual players and so forth.

'The plan is to be in the top six when the League splits. The bigger picture for me is the Atlantic League. I think it will happen and I want to be the third Scottish club playing against the Benficas and Ajax. I think we would do well in Europe. Between Dario and Ivano they've been in three European Cup finals.

'As far as the stadium goes, Jimmy and I have put something like three million pounds in. Banks look at football clubs as liabilities and for them to find the £800,000 we needed was tough. We got help from Gavin Masterton of the Bank of Scotland, who was chairman of Dunfermline, and he pointed us in the direction of finance companies. The unfortunate thing was that Dunfermline were then relegated. But that's football.

'For two or three years, I've been watching Real Mallorca. Five or six years ago they were the same as Dundee but a family took them over and have been very clever. They are involved with a Spanish agency which has six offices in South America. Now, every year, they sell on two or three players and that's what we'll have to do to cover the losses on players' wages. You must have the contacts to bring in players to replace those who will be saleable to other clubs. We'll never be a huge club – but we could be one of the top Scottish clubs. Douglas covered last year's loss, but we have to do this every year. There's nothing new about it: United sold a player just about every year to balance the books.

'As far as amalgamation goes, you have to look past the city. If we amalgamate, who is big enough to replace the team that goes? We can both be successful at a certain level but, in the bigger picture, a joint stadium is where we'd cut our costs. In future, we're all going to be operating from training camps with soccer academies. I think we should get private money involved and build a stadium for both clubs which is more accessible. Let's say we each need to spend £4 million. The £8 million would be better spent on a new joint stadium with easier access. As far as ground-sharing goes, no one has made that kind of approach to the SPL. It wouldn't happen in Glasgow but in Edinburgh or Dundee maybe? And then there's the bigger picture again: Scotland might get the European Championship in 2008 and we'll need a 30,000 capacity. I think 15–20,000 is better for the clubs, but we could plan with temporary, additional stands in mind.'

TEN

SEASON 2000–01

Up wi' the Bonettis

Following pre-season training in Italy and two friendlies against Raith Rovers and Grimsby, it was the opinion of the *Courier* sportswriter Dan Stewart that whatever the 2000–01 campaign held, it would not be dull. Ivano was confident that the young Scots in the team would benefit and that the team, overall, would do well. His first signing, the amazingly talented Georgian captain and midfield creator, Nemsadze, was already conjuring up memories of Charlie Cooke and was on his way to similar cult status, while the Argentinian forwards Caballero (squat and powerful) and Sara (quick and good in the air) looked a very promising combination. Marrocco appeared to be a very skilful wing-back and his fellow Italian De Marchi was a central defender with a good touch.

The Bonettis, Ivano (born in 1964) and Dario (born in 1961), had come originally from the town of Brescia near Verona in northern Italy and both had played at the very highest levels of European football with clubs such as Juventus, Sampdoria, Roma and AC Milan. Their management experience (Sestrese, once described to me as Vauxhall Conference) was limited, but both obviously brought a young lifetime's thought and experience to the game and their contacts were international. Their playing strategy, broadly speaking, was to bring the very best international players they could at a price (principally wages, no transfer fees if possible) their employers could afford. The game would then be played 'Latin-style' for want of a better description, with everyone required to be comfortable on the ball and able to link defence with attack by quick control and one-touch football when necessary. The notion of Scots aggression (and skill) would also be accommodated by one or two players in each area. Given some of the negativities of the Scottish game, it was an incredibly bold move by all concerned.

The curtain came up in Motherwell on 29 July and,

straightaway, the 2,000 travelling fans who had begun to fly Italian, Argentinian and Spanish flags – not to mention the Motherwell support – could see that something special was afoot. Bonetti, a physically committed player as well as a technically gifted one, was unfortunately ordered off with two yellow cards, but a first-half goal from Billio and an Artero wonder-run and finish gave Dundee a 2–0 victory.

The Dundee FC team comprised: Douglas, Smith, Tweed, di Marchi (Italy), Marrocco (Italy), Billio (Italy), Artero (Spain), Nemsadze (Georgia), Bonetti (Italy), Sara and Caballero (both Argentina).

The second match was a home game against Dunfermline, who were now managed by Jimmy Nicholl and Jimmy Calderwood, a Scot who had spent time in the Dutch game. Within 12 seconds the Mighty Pars had lost an own goal, and penalties from Sara and Caballero gave Dundee a 3–0 victory in front of a 7,100 crowd – 6,000 of whom were Dundee fans. 'Nemsadze ran the game,' said Calderwood. Juan Sara revealed himself as a committed Christian, by showing a 'Jesus loves you' message on his T-shirt after his goal. Such displays would become his trademark.

Dundee now topped the League and at least one fan was known to have placed a substantial bet on them to lift the title. It was slightly premature, however, and both Caballero and the team as a whole came crashing down to earth in the next match at Easter Road. Alex McLeish had put together a good mix of youth, experience, skill and graft since bringing his side up from the First Division and a 3–0 victory over United the previous week had led to the resignation of Paul Sturrock. Again prompted by Nemsadze, however, Caballero cracked in a great right-foot shot in 12 minutes to open the scoring, before the Dark Blues succumbed to two great solo goals by Didier Agathe. The game was still open, however, when Matthius Jack caught Caballero in the corner and put him up in the air with a two-footed tackle. The Argentinian then appeared to strike the German on the way down, and was red-carded. This killed the game as a spectacle and eventually Dundee were reduced to nine men when Billio was also sent off. They lost 5–1.

Two thousand Dundee supporters had again travelled to the match and the fans' grief was compounded when McLeish and one of his players complained of 'Latin temperament', shown in players falling down when given the slightest touch. Dundee, legitimately, complained of racial stereotyping but in some ways the psychological damage was done and in the next two games, against St Mirren (1–2) and Hearts (1–1), the club continued to suffer injury, red cards and penalties. A 1–1 draw at home to Rangers steadied the ship somewhat, and more players arrived in the shape of Italian Alessandro Romano and Argentinian Walter Del Rio, but trouble refused to go away and, in the next match – a CIS Cup game, again at Love Street – things began to look more serious. Both Billio and Wilkie were red-carded, there were six bookings and the game was lost 3–0.

'I am looking to God,' said Ivano.

Actually, the Dundee manager was also taking a more reasoned approach. He requested an informal meeting with the SFA and a briefing by ex-Dundee ref Bob Valentine and anounced that he would be taking some advice from the Chelsea manager, Gianlucca Vialli (who, ironically, was on the point of losing his own job).

The match against St Johnstone at MacDiarmid Park was a rather dull one with goalkeeper Douglas coming to the rescue late in the game. Bonetti acknowledged, however, that the football had been good in the first 20 minutes and it was a case of converting this into goals. Goals finally came in the first Dundee derby, at Dens Park. United dominated the first half, but a second-half hat-trick by Sara carried the game – although Caballero was badly injured in a three-way clash with Jason De Vos and Kevin McDonald. Both Dario and Ivano became embroiled in the subsequent controversy. Ivano, in the heat of the moment, said that United were the worst team for dishonest tackling he had ever played against, but he later tempered his views. Caballero,

LEFT:
Ivano Bonetti,
a skilful and physically
committed player.

BELOW:
Peter and Jimmy Marr.
Chief executive and
Chairman – unlikely
revolutionaries.

ABOVE:
A new coaching challenge for two stars of Italian
football, Dario and Ivano Bonetti.

Claudio Caniggia, the Argentinian 'Bird', still a
world-class player.

Robert Douglas, a fine young goalkeeper and the
first major transfer (to Celtic).

Jamie Langfield, the young Scotland squad keeper, saves from Jim Hamiilton.

Barry Smith, club captain under three managers.

LEFT:
Zurab Khizanishvili, a great young talent who followed Nemsadze from Georgia.

CENTRE:
Walter Del Rio – wholehearted commitment in a variety of positions.

ABOVE:
Beto Carranza – brilliant quicksilver Argentinian.

Gavin Rae, Scottish International and powerhouse of the midfield.

Georgi Nemsadze and Javier Artero. The Georgian captain and his Spanish teammate brought class to the midfield.

Juan Sara (above)
and Fabian
Caballero (left).
The Argentinian
strikeforce has
shown great
potential, although
injury has often
kept them apart.

Temuri Ketsbaia, an exciting Georgian midfielder.

Fan Zhiyi, centre-back and Chinese International captain.

The backroom
boys – business
manager Jim
Connor (above)
and club
co-ordinator
Dario Magri
(right).

however, would be out of action for some months. It was said that only his particular muscle strength had prevented a leg break. Ivano needed a replacement striker.

In a moment of inspiration Ivano decided to try his friend again, the Argentinian World Cup star Claudio Caniggia, who had apparently turned down a move earlier in the season. By now, however, relations had deteriorated further with his club Boca Juniors and it was a disbelieving world which witnessed Maradona's former strike partner arrive at Dens for a photocall on 4 October. It was even said that Maradona himself might drop in, some time in the future! The long-haired Caniggia signed up with another Argentinian, the attacking midfielder Beto Carranza, but neither was able to play in the next game, a rather dull 0–0 draw at home to Kilmarnock.

The world of Dundee Football Club would not, however, be dull in the weeks and months to come. Taking the number 33 (which approximately matched his age), Caniggia – 'the Bird', or '*el Pajaro*' (pronounced 'el Pachro') as he was known in Argentina – immediately triggered a commercial bonanza of replica shirts and made his debut at Aberdeen on 14 October. The Dundee fans, many sporting long blond wigs, took up their entire allocation of tickets (2,500) and welcomed Caniggia at the start of the second half. Although suffering the predictable harsh tackling (Gavin Rae was also sent off), he immediately showed his class with some delightful touches and added a late goal to Ivano's earlier one, a clever chip, to give Dundee a 2–0 victory.

These events were overshadowed somewhat by an incident back at Tannadice where, following a 4–0 home defeat by Hearts, United chairman Jim McLean had assaulted a BBC reporter and resigned. But praise for Claudio was still effusive. He was 'Dundee's biggest signing since Billy Steel' said the *Courier*. Ivano compared it to Roberto Baggio's move to Bologna. And commercial manager Jim Connor described it as something which would bring not only playing benefits but also commercial rewards to the club. The

Argentinian himself said he was pleased to be working with Ivano and Dario again, having known them in Italy. He was not here just to pick up the wages. The football, passing and intelligence would give him a platform to get back into the Argentinian national side. The physical side of the Scottish game concerned him a little, but a man needed ambition and this was what he had found in Dundee.

Briefly, Caniggia's career had taken him from River Plate in Buenos Aires, to Verona then Atalanta (Bergamo) and Roma (where he was suspended for cocaine use), then Benfica and back to Boca Juniors in Argentina, with whom he was now, apparently, in dispute (this would not be difficult to believe – the Argentinian economy was in particularly bad shape at the time). Arguably, the highlight of his footballing career was the 1990 World Cup where, as Maradona's strike partner, he scored the only goal of the game to beat Brazil in the quarter-final (I don't know if I can comprehend what that would make him to football fans in Argentina. A deity?), scored again in the semi against Italy, and played in the final against Germany.

Well – now he was in Dundee and the days promised excitement indeed. But at what price? Peter Marr was not hanging about. He had earlier stated that the club was still looking to progress on a number of fronts, not least ground-sharing, but he was also honest enough to say that they were taking a big gamble – Caniggia's wage alone was rumoured to be £10,000 per week, including perks such as TV rights and they would have to sell players. The outstanding young goalkeeper Robert Douglas would be first and, within the week, he was on his way to Celtic for a fee in excess of £1 million.

All this high finance contrasted sharply with a deal which was being discussed at Arbroath Football Club that same week. The club was swithering on an 'expensive' deal for ex-United player Grant Johnston, whose terms were reported as £30 per week basic, £20 appearance money, a £10,000 signing-on fee at £200 per week, plus relocation money and a win bonus. Mark you, as Dan

Stewart pointed out in the *Courier*, it was not that long since Dundee had been trading tracksuits for a Fife junior.

Douglas's immediate replacement was his deputy Jamie Langfield, but the young goalie had something of a nightmare start, losing two goals in the first five minutes against Motherwell in what was Caniggia's home debut. Dundee fans had taken up 7,000 of the 8,500 home tickets available. At least they witnessed another magical, chipped goal from the striker, and sympathy was expressed for Langfield who had been exposed, in a sense, by central defender Wilkie's inexperience. Ivano knew what had to be done and a young Italian goalkeeper, Marco Rocatti, was signed on loan from Bologna, as Peter Marr headed for Australia to check out a possible commercial tie-up with an Aussie club.

Rocatti made his debut on a snowy Saturday in Dunfermline. Caniggia's presence, though, had encouraged the American cable network ESPN to relay the match to Argentina too and this trend would accelerate in future with Dundee games going live to Australia, New Zealand, the US and the Caribbean. Bonetti's tactic for the Pars game was to play Claudio as a lone striker, backed up by the midfield until later in the game when another forward might come on. It worked after a fashion, but Cannigia's lay-offs inevitably fell to non-strikers such as Smith and Rae and a late header by David Moss of Dunfermline took the points (1–0).

The Bonettis were obviously puzzled by these defeats and Dario called for greater concentration in order to finish off opponents. The exhortation fell on deaf ears, however, for in the very next game against Hibs at Dens, a match shown on Sky TV, Billio managed to play a pass-back into no man's land between Tweed and Rocatti which resulted in a scrambled goal. Tweed equalised but Hibs' Zitelli won the match with a good overhead strike (which was later almost replicated by Sara).

This meant that Dundee had lost the last three games by one goal, and Ivano was not having it. Billio was dropped and subsequently told that he would be allowed to move on. Falconer would stay as Caniggia's partner (in spite of Sara's earlier goals against United). This immediately paid off at Tannadice when the big striker's pass gave Claudio another goal. The match was sealed (2–0) by a brilliant chip, this time from Nemsadze. It was the first time that Dundee had gained three straight victories over United since their championship year of 1961–62.

Caniggia now offered to extend his stay – citing the beautiful Tay sunsets as one reason, and the fact that his son was attending a Dundee primary school. Bonetti was glowing in praise of his Scottish players. 'In Italy,' he said, 'attitudes would not have been so positive. All the players are learning from one another.'

On 18 November, Dundee gave one of their finest performances to crush St Mirren 5–0. The Buddies were, admittedly, holding up the League with United but had won the earlier encounters against the Dark Blues so the emphatic result was a measure of progress. Caniggia scored twice, with Rae and Milne getting one each, but none was better that the fourth, finished by Artero. Playing the ball to the byline, the big Spaniard (who bears an uncanny resemblance to the young Bobby Seith) took the return on the penalty spot and tapped it passed the Saints' goalie. It was Caniggia's reverse pass which brought the crowd to its feet, however, and TV footage revealed a glorious moment which encapsulated Claudio's genius. As he whips round on the byline and rolls the ball back to Artero in one movement, the entire St Mirren defence is seen lumbering in the wrong direction, away from the ball. Magic.

Dundee now sat sixth in the League and with games against a manager-less Hearts side at Tynecastle and one against St Johnstone at Dens to come, there was obvious potential for consolidation of that position. Unfortunately, it was a case of 'best-laid schemes . . .'. As in their previous visit to Edinburgh, the Dark Blues scored first, through a blistering Carranza free-kick (Beto had replaced Nemsadze who had felt ill during the warm-up.) In the second half, however, they were overhauled, first by a Murray header then by two late goals from Colin Cameron.

BONETTI'S BLUES

The match at Dens against the Perth Saints was another late horror show. Sara scored in the first half with a looping header before Tweed went off with a head knock. His deputy, Wilkie, came on to play a very steady game and Dundee had plenty of chances to kill the game but, with the last kick of the match, Sylla swept over a cross which Connolly got a touch to, and the ball came off Wilkie's chest before ricocheting between him and the goalkeeper and going into the net.

The Dens fans went home seriously depressed and they might even have had suicidal tendencies by the time another last-gasp touch gave Celtic the points at the next home match, once again televised live by Sky. This time, however, there was nothing but praise for the Dark Blues and for Caniggia in particular, who had an outstanding game. Falling behind to an early Petrov strike, Dundee proceeded to dominate the middle period of the match and equalised when a probing second-half cross from Claudio was put into his own net by Tom Boyd. Once again there was a last-minute ricochet – this time between Chris Coyne (who had replaced the injured de Marchi) and Tweed – and once again there was a last-touch goal from Agathe (who was now a Bhoy).

The Glasgow press were fulsome in their praise of Dundee. The same people who had ridiculed the Caniggia transfer were now falling over each other to praise the team and suggest that the Argentinian might be the solution to Rangers' current problems! (Piss off. I mean, everyone has his price but this quick cheque-book fix rarely works for the buyer, who is merely demonstrating a lack of imagination and would have had serious consequences for the seller at this stage in this case.)

Dundee were now five points behind St Johnstone and Hearts and lying in an (unthinkable) seventh position. 'The highly regarded but occasionally casual' Wilkie (as he was described by *Courier* journalist Graeme Dey) was also in trouble with Bonetti and might, it was said, go out on loan. But Ivano himself was trying to keep the players focused on the next match, which was away to

Kilmarnock. Caniggia would miss this because he had to return to face Boca Juniors on a legal matter.

He was replaced by young Steven Milne and when Killie went two up with goals at the beginning of each half, it looked as if it was all over. Miraculously, however, Gordon Marshall fumbled a Bonetti shot and Milne then rattled in two – one from a clever Falconer dummy and another following a piece of Artero magic on the right wing. Both Hearts and St Johnstone lost, so the Tayzurri were back in business.

Chris Coyne was now beginning to make some impact in central defence and a highly rated young Georgian with the commentator's nightmare name of Zurab Khizanishvili was said to be thinking about a move to Dens. He was a free agent because his club, Lokomotiv Tbilisi, had gone out of business and the prospect of teaming up with his national captain Nemsadze made Dundee an attractive proposition. The next game was against Aberdeen at Dens. Once again the first goal went to the opposition through a lack of concentration in central defence. A good penalty claim was turned down when Caniggia was barged in the box by Solberg and the Argentinian was booked for protesting, but Dundee slowly took control of the game and were ahead with goals from Sara and Carranza when a very dubious penalty was given against Barry Smith for pushing in the box. It seemed as though the ref was the only one who saw it.

Just after Christmas, Dundee were back in the top six with a 3–0 win at Motherwell – although Caniggia was missing and Marrocco was sent off. The team at this point was Rocatti, Del Rio, Marrocco, Tweed, Smith, Carranza, Nemsadze, Rae, McSkimming, Sara and Milne. Sara scored two and Rae one, with a good headed goal. Back at Dens, the home match against Dunfermline was postponed due to a frozen pitch. Victory here would have set the Dark Blues up nicely before the break, but it wasn't to be and Hibs gave them another sound defeat (3–0) in the last match. Laursen was given space on the left and Steven Tweed misjudged the flight of the ball to let Paatelainen score with a header. A scrambled goal made it two just before the interval and an O'Neill shot was deflected past Rocatti in the second half. The Italian goalkeeper then left the field through injury and Langfield did well as his deputy, making at least one top-class save.

Bonetti's summary of the first half of the season was that the Dens revolution had only just begun. He thought the team had played some high-quality football but had needlessly lost around eight points, and no one would argue with that. There was also unanimity about looking forward to the partnership of Caniggia and Caballero and, although this would take longer than anticipated to materialise, there was cheering news for the fans when Peter Marr announced that Claudio had signed a two-and-a-half-year extension to his contract. It was the largest amount ever invested in a Dundee player, said Marr, and Claudio had signed it without even consulting his agent.

'The Dundee of Scotland where Caniggia plays wants that Diego plays in Dubai . . . so we are to go to Dubai,' said Diego Maradona, according to the appropriately named Babel Fish translation service during the winter break. Then it was reported that the 'Hand of God' would be coming to Dens Park to play in a friendly with Napoli as opposition. Imagination was spiralling out of control . . .

> *And now, the world's most famous footballer, Diego Maradona, finally enters the home dressing-room at Dens Park and reaches for that famous Dark Blue jersey bearing the immortal legend CERAMIC TILE WAREHOUSE . . .*

Of course it would have been a commercial circus (although I have no doubt that Caniggia could indeed facilitate such an event).

Gavin Rae extended his contract, Lee Wilkie went on loan to Plymouth Argyle (now managed by Paul Sturrock) and the team headed once more to their training camp in the north of Italy. The fans remembered that the Dark Blues had come out of the traps like greyhounds following their previous stint in Riccione, but it was not to be repeated.

The first match on their return was a Scottish Cup game against First Division Falkirk. The game at Dens was drawn, but Dundee got through 2–0 in the replay at Brockville. Then came United at Dens and the Dark Blue motivation was now seriously being questioned as they went down 2–3 to the Terrors with Bonetti saying that the result flattered his (slightly depleted) team. Rae and Sara both missed the match due to suspension and Bonetti tore a calf muscle, but things were now going from bad to worse. Or even bad to weird.

The next match was against bottom team St Mirren at Love Street. Dundee were completely in control and Sara scored in the first half. When he ran to show the St Mirren fans his T-shirt with its religious message, however, he was booked, and then sent off for an innocuous hand ball. Six minutes later, St Mirren equalised and they won the game with a late goal. Bonetti was bemused, furious and critical of the inconsistency of refereeing, as Sara had been allowed his demonstration in previous matches and other players appeared to celebrate in much the same way.

The rumour mill continued to grind: Benito Carbone was coming from Bradford; Dundee were to play in the Inter Toto Cup (they had not been in Europe since 1974); and Sara and Caballero were to be the subject of expensive transfer fees at the end of their first season. Dundee met Hearts in the fourth round of the Cup and came away from Tynecastle with a creditable 1–1 draw, Rocatti having saved a Cameron penalty. In the rearranged League match, however, they went down 1–0 to Dunfermline at home and thus had taken no points from three lowly teams that they must have been expecting to beat. Peter Marr tried to take some of the heat off by saying that a 'best club in Tayside' would suffice for the first year but it didn't really wash and the fans were now seriously worried about that top-six place. The bizarre stuff continued. Rangers came to Dens and gave away two penalties. Sara missed them both and Dodds missed one for Rangers before Konterman scored the winner. Five straight League defeats. Would the Cup bring satisfaction?

The bad League run was halted before the Hearts replay when Dundee travelled to Perth and come away with a fighting 3–2 win. It was a game of errors but, following a Gary Bollan goal direct from a free-kick, Rae equalised with a great strike and Sara made it 2–1. Sara had his critics, but he certainly got the goals. De Marchi gave away a penalty which was converted, but Artero – another man who has worked tirelessly over the season – got a late winner. 'We had to win this,' said Bonetti. 'It was our last chance for top six.' There would, however, be more drama to come before the SPL split.

Wednesday, 7 March 2001
Dundee versus Hearts:
Scottish Cup Fourth-Round Replay

It's a beautiful day and I travel to Dundee with excitement, in anticipation of one of these great Wednesday night matches, in spite of recent results. In what can only be described as an act of cultural homage, I decide to visit the Deep Sea Fish Restaurant in the Nethergate, the Harry Ramsden's of Dundee. The Italian connection is there of course and the family have been in the business in the town for generations (writing this I am reminded of my family friend Ciano Soave, the Haparanda café and Dundee musician Benny Esposito, who was known in the vernacular as 'Benny Eh suppose so'), although the first (Deep Sea) restaurant was across the road and my personal memory is of 'busters' – chips and slightly mushy, marrowfat peas usually taken with vinegar – in the upper, rear part of the old place. In the '50s, my parents would take my sister and myself to the Palace Variety Theatre on an occasional Wednesday night and a visit to the Deep Sea served to heighten the pleasure.

Tonight I order fish, chips, a portion of peas and a cup of tea and I'm slightly disconcerted when the diminutive waitress (they were always classic wee Dundee wifies) calls to the frier 'one supper!'. A supper, I surmise, must be code for what I have asked for. I go to the downstairs toilet to wash my hands and, when I return, two or three tables around mine have also been filled, one by a mother and baby. Time goes by, I read the *Evening Telegraph* – another important cultural component on such occasions.

After a brief eternity, the table next to me gets four fish suppers. The mother and baby then get spaghetti bolognese. The waitress picks up on my slightly despairing look and turns to the frier. 'Eh'm still waitin' on one,' she calls.

'How can that be?' asks the frier. I recognise him as the boss, one of the brothers who were teenagers in the '50s and early '60s.

'Cos eh am!' is the retort.

I want to shout, 'Never mind a' this – eh'm stervin'!'

The waitress comes over.

'Sorry aboot this,' she says, 'he's on his way . . . eh, *it's* on its way.'

Another two minutes. Suddenly, up comes fish and chips only, and horror must now be written on my face.

'Dinna worry,' she reassures me, 'yer tea's on its way.'

'No, it was the *peas*,' I protest, limply.

She turns on her heels and calls 'One portion o' peas!'

'Wha's that fur?' asks the chef?

'!*^$!@£*! *Me*!' I want to scream.

An elderly man approaches my table. 'Kin eh borrie yer pipper?' he asks.

'Yes, of course.' (Nae peas, nae tea, nae *Tele* . . .)

The waitress returns with full complement. 'Sorry aboot that.'

Ahh . . . delicious.

At the Snug Bar in Caldrum Street, I meet two old school friends, David Pollington and Gordon Wishart, who are both now senior DC Thomson journalists, and in the Dens Stand there's another, Ronnie Scott, who writes on sport for the *Sunday Post*. Unfortunately, the game serves only to reinforce the pattern of weirdness which continues to afflict the Bonetti team. Just as the Dark Blues are getting on top of Hearts, Gavin Rae is badly fouled by Lee Makel and the next thing we know, Marco de Marchi is sent off. He has apparently become involved right under the referee's nose and the linesman sees him kick the Hearts player. Making his familiar praying gesture, de Marchi tries to leave the field near the Dundee dugout. Bonetti pointedly ignores him in a way that suggests the defender's time at Dens is coming to an end. Sure enough, although the ten-man Dundee play well, they lose to a headed goal by Tomaschek and miss out on a £500,000 payday at Celtic Park in the quarter-finals. Nothing is done in the immediate future, since the popular DFC kit man Willie Dryden dies the next day. By the Friday, however, Bonetti has cut de Marchi loose. He states frankly that the Italian deserved to be sent off and that he can no longer trust a player who lets him down in this way in a big game. A Hearts supporter speaking to me in Glasgow compliments the Dundee manager on his refreshing honesty and candour, not least because 'Dundee were gonna win that game'.

Zurab Khizanishvili had by now been signed (along with Aussie Mark Robertson) and Nemsadze said the young Georgian would be as good as Rio Ferdinand (who had just been transferred to Leeds from West Ham for £18 million). I expect that cheered up the Dens accountants. Something was obviously boosting morale, for Dundee now went to Ibrox and won 2–0 with goals from Caniggia and Milne. The team featured a new Argentinian, Beto Garrido, who, like Romano, looked comfortable in the midfield. Caballero was also back in training but the Dee could not keep the form going and next drew 0–0 with Hearts at Dens in a poor game. Unbelievably, snow was still affecting games (which cannot have cheered up the foreign contingent much). It was four months since Dundee had won at home.

Caniggia was SPL Player of the Month and Jocky Scott was Division Two Manager of the Month with Notts County in England. Also, the superb architecture of Morgan Academy was destroyed by fire; and Chesterfield were rebuffed by the Marrs over a proposed (and unlikely) business link-up between the two clubs. Gavin Rae was called up by Scotland – a fitting compliment to a player who had had an excellent season – and Zurab Khizanishvili got his work permit.

All this, however, paled as the final week before the split arrived. Dundee drew with Kilmarnock at Dens then lost a close game to Celtic at Parkhead. Rumours of Caniggia's departure to one of the Old Firm clubs were gaining unwelcome momentum but the transfer deadline passed and the SPL was beautifully poised for a final day of drama. If Celtic could beat St Mirren they would win the League – and they duly did. For Dundee fans, however, there were two completely different centres of attention: Dunfermline were three points ahead and playing Kilmarnock away. Dundee were at Pittodrie and had to win – and have Kilmarnock beat Dunfermline – to get that top-six place. Miraculously, and in what seemed like the first piece of luck in ages, Dundee won 2–0 with goals from Nemsadze and Caballero (who had replaced the injured Caniggia) and Killie survived a late onslaught to beat the Pars. The last ten minutes were the most excruciating I can remember as the 'double' came tantalisingly closer. The suspense at Pitoddrie was captured, as TV cameras and players focused on the fans who were huddling round those tuned into Radio Scotland.

'Mission accomplished', the DFC website read the following day, and even the *Sunday Post* exclusive which revealed that Caniggia would definitely sign for Rangers at the end of the season could not dampen spirits. The project was on course. The adventure would continue.

ELEVEN

SO, FAREWELL THEN, CLAUDIO . . .

BONETTI'S BLUES

I have never been to Argentina but I presume that its Spanish cultural links and historic connections with fascist dictators make it not unlike Iberia in many ways. Anyone who visited Spain during Franco's time will testify to what the combination of a determined, right-wing generalissimo and an unforgiving landscape can reduce a people to. In the '60s and early '70s, even magnificent cities like Barcelona and Valencia were drab and cowed places where the police strutted around like film stars and the most prosperous-looking businesses and families in the community appeared to be connected to private medicine in some way. In the developing holiday trade, ordinary people worked for pennies (literally) and what I saw of their homes when hitchhiking was a humbling experience. Rough, home-made furniture, primitive water and toilet facilities, and pretty basic food (albeit imaginatively served by lovely people).

Go to the Spanish cities now or, indeed, the holiday resorts and you see vibrant communities of physically handsome people building aggressively for the future and a living testament to democracy and even European union. Critically, in the real Spanish towns, kids still play football in the streets and anyone watching the Spanish Goal of the Month on TV nowadays gets the idea of what this ultimately can lead to in terms of skill allied to athleticism and all-year-round sunshine.

What this has to do with Claudio Caniggia is that when I see him careering through a defence, fearless and precariously balanced as if on a wall of death while great hulking defenders think about crunching into him, but not daring to for fear of the penalty, I can imagine him learning his trade on the rough streets and parks of Buenos Aires. I suspect, like Glasgow's blaze pitches, if you could control a ball at high speed on these types of surfaces whilst awaiting the retribution of defenders unhampered by referees, you would be ready for anything.

What I really marvel at with Caniggia is that he rarely does anything without adding something constructive to his team's play:

if he runs, there's a gap; if he jumps, even with a much taller man, he often gets a touch; if he's caught in a tight corner he frequently manages to secure a pass or a throw, off a defender.

Then there's the walk. He initially struck me as some kind of prehistoric, grounded flying animal and to discover that his nickname was *El Pajaro* (the Bird) was a great delight, although the 'Vulture' or 'Pterodactyl' would also have worked. I've since discovered that the name was actually given because Caniggia 'flies', and his phenomenal quickness and speed of thought is, of course, his greatest asset.

When the Leagues divided, the papers were full of the 'Caniggia for Rangers' story and one ventured that the forward's hamstring injury might be of a more diplomatic nature when Rangers came to Dens for the first game. Sure enough, he didn't play, but virtually a full house turned out for yet another weird game which showed up Dundee's recurring weaknesses. Nemsadze, in many ways, was the star player on the park and brilliantly carved his way past three or four players, only to hit a fierce shot straight at Klos. Rangers went up the field and a defensive error let Wallace in for a goal. Within minutes, a Carranza dummy gave Sara an open goal. Klos saved, put the ball up the park, defensive ineptitude, 0–2. Again Dundee came forward, and again Sara received the ball in front of the goal. There was a miscue and Klos saved from Rae. What happened next? You guessed it. Albertz shot and it finished 0–3. The only bright spot was Zurab at right-back: an outstanding prospect and another coup for Bonetti.

The Caniggia story now went into overdrive. The player (or his agent) seemed to think he was free to move. Peter Marr disagreed but said that the right price would secure Claudio's transfer. The west–coast press were literally drooling and managed to find pictures of Caniggia's son in a Celtic strip and his wife in her birthday suit. Then Rangers maintained they had no interest. Then they lost 3–0 to Celtic at Ibrox.

Dundee, meanwhile, met Hibs at Dens. The Dark Blues had

been three-time losers to the Edinburgh side and Caniggia played but, two defensive errors later, it was four times (0–2). 'I know what is wrong,' said Ivano, 'and I will fix it for next year.' The changes appeared to include Zurab going into central defence and this contributed to a long-awaited Dens Park victory the following week, against Kilmarnock.

Sara, and Carranza from a penalty, gave Dundee a 2–1 win – the first at home since November – and although it did not really improve Dundee's European chances, the next game certainly improved their morale. There was also a funny moment when Sara went forward to claim the ball for the penalty. Given his recent record, he was spontaneously surrounded by the whole team saying, 'Haud oan, amigo [or words to that effect]. Jesus may indeed love you but this is no' your baw.'

The penultimate game was against Celtic at Parkhead on a beautiful, sunny May day. Caniggia's transfer was still incomplete but he was now certain to go to Rangers and unlikely to pull on a Dundee shirt again. Bonetti decided to go with Caballero on his own up front and a pairing of Zurab and Coyne in central defence, but, as had happened all season, the plan was immediately thrown into chaos when the young Georgian was sent off following an innocuous challenge with Larsson. Dundee fans feared the worst, especially as Nemsadze was absent for compassionate reasons but, almost immediately, the team went forward and Fabian scored with a good first touch and turn. Then, before half time he made it two, following uncertainty in the Celtic box. The eventual 2–0 victory proved to be Celtic's only home defeat of the season. Jamie Langfield also did his prospects no harm with the only shut-out to be seen at Parkhead over the same period.

Dundee's final match of an amazing season was at Tynecastle. Caballero was once again in a lone forward role. A number of players – Del Rio, Romano, Garrido, Carranza – showed their utility value by playing in slightly different positions. Hearts won the game 2–0. The most amazing thing, however, was the fans' performance. With ten or fifteen minutes to go and the game lost, the substantial travelling support began to sing 'Ivano . . . Dario' in mock opera style and, to everyone's astonishment, this carried on until well beyond the final whistle. It was a strange and wonderful conclusion to a strange and wonderful season. Dundee finished sixth. Celtic won the domestic treble in Martin O'Neill's first season.

Caniggia finally revealed his decision to go to Rangers and Dundee got £1 million, although it was rumoured that they had to split the fee with the striker and, significantly, that his wages would be *doubled* at Ibrox, to £6,000 per week. Earlier in the season Claudio was said to be getting up to £18,000 a week, but it is much more likely that a more realistic basic wage was paid, with add-ons from TV, commercial and sell-on rights.

The season is no sooner over than the Dark Blues are limbering up for a return to Europe. Peter Marr and Ivano have taken a decision to enter the Inter-Toto Cup, a European rabbits' event, success in which will bring entry to the UEFA Cup. It means a gamble in terms of inadequate rest before the new season, but everyone appears to be up for it, notwithstanding the fact that the draw pairs them with Sartid of Yugoslavia, a politically tough cookie.

There is the usual close-season skirmishing in the press: de Marchi and Billio remain in contractual limbo, Roccati returns to Bologna, a Scottish European Championship bid puts Dundee and United's ground-sharing back on the agenda, Gavin Rae and Lee Wilkie are said to be interesting Everton and Leeds respectively, and Juan Sara's contractual position is causing some concern. All this is forgotten, however, when the European flags return to Dens after an absence of 27 years. The game attracts a respectable 7,000 crowd, including 20 Serbians, but it is a towsy, unattractive and goalless affair. Dundee have the better of the game and the midfield (inspired by Romano), plus the defensive pairing of Coyne and Wilkie both look good. The team fails to score, however, and – still without Nemsadze, Zurab and Carranza – must take up the challenge again in Belgrade.

There, disaster strikes. Caballero puts the Blues ahead but then two soft penalties knock the stuffing out of the team and they go in 3–1 down. Sara brings them back to 3–2 in 75 minutes, so the 'victory draw' is on when Caballero gets sent off. The game finishes 5–2 with Bonetti protesting about the competence of the non-English-speaking Bulgarian referee.

The out-of-favour Dutchman Frank van Eis now returned to his native shores saying, 'I could write a book about what I have seen at this club.'

I know the feeling.

TWELVE

JIMMY MARR: CHAIRMAN

BONETTI'S BLUES

To Peter, me and the supporters – it's in our hearts.

I took a little tour of my old stamping ground on the day I interviewed the Dundee chairman and, to be frank, the place did not look to be in very great shape. The fact that Morgan Academy had largely burned down in the recent fire did not augur well but there was at least evidence of architectural salvaging going on, suggesting that the school would be restored to former glory. Unfortunately the same could not be said for the Baxter Park bandstand, broken down and covered by graffiti, although I was pleased to see that the tennis courts were still being used. The 'Glebie' was still there but Baxter Park church had been replaced by flats, the jute mills had been semi-demolished and the Princess Street/Albert Street area looked terminally run down. Where, I wonder, do the local people find community? Pubs?

Given this backdrop, Jimmy Marr might be seen as an inspirational figure. Possibly Scottish football's youngest chairman, he certainly is an unlikely character, refreshingly shunning the limelight and evidently more interested in the nuts and bolts of he and his brother's business empire which currently employs 500 people in the city and turns over perhaps £12 million per annum. He had also, that week, opened an Irish-style bar in Lochee and named it after his granny, Ellen Shannon, who was the first of his family to come over from Ireland at the turn of the century and who herself had lived and worked in Lochee.

He told me: 'I was always a Dundee supporter but I didn't play much because I wasn't any good. I served my time as a painter and decorator with a local company and when Peter got involved with pubs I worked part-time and then I got the tenancy of the Hawthorn at the bottom of the Hilltown which I ran myself. This is still the pattern today: Peter runs his companies, the construction and children's nurseries; I have mine [a chain of pubs] and we come together on certain projects, like the football club and a property company.

'Peter also had a string of nursing homes which he sold on and for the next couple of years (for tax reasons) he will be based in Mallorca. He comes back for the home games, arriving on a Friday and leaving on the Monday. Peter is in daily contact with both the club and Ivano, so he still does a lot although he's in Spain. He also enjoys the press side of things – which I don't – and the direct contact is done through Beattie Media and Damon Rhind. We made the mistake of not appointing anybody in this area at the beginning and paid for it over the John McCormack business. Otherwise we try to run the club on a family basis, everyone knows each other by first names and there must be 75 to 100 full-time people between the playing and admin staff. In total, Peter and I will be employing around 500 and turning over maybe ten to twelve million pounds.

'This is good for the corporate side of the club. We can go through lists of suppliers and they are receptive to helping out at Dens Park although when we got involved at first with Dundee, a number of local business people said, if we got control, they would help with this and that and now they've run a mile. It's disappointing, and yet there's our shirt sponsor Jim Miller from Ceramic Tile Warehouse. He's Kirkcaldy born and bred and totally supportive, to the extent that he tiled the stand facilities. You'd think we'd have found a local sponsor. Having said that, the fan in the street has done his bit, buying bricks and taking up the share issue. Our season tickets are now over 5,000 and I would like to know when that happened last. The figure was 600 when we arrived.

'When Peter first got involved with Tayport Juniors I was just a fan and sponsor. I would go to Dens and Tannadice and I'd sponsor Peter's players through the pubs, and also at St Joseph's. But I wasn't as committed to football as Peter was and our relations were good because we were doing our own thing. We did the

Mardi Gras nightclub together; Peter built it and I ran it on a day-to-day basis. As one of the most successful nightclubs in Scotland, it gave us the cash to take on Dundee FC.

'We were despairing over the situation at Dens when Cook and Dixon were involved – things were quite bleak. Jim Connor and Derek Souter were helping on the commercial side at St Joseph's. Derek had also been an employee of Dundee FC but his dismissal had led to a long-running legal dispute which was going to cost Dundee a lot of money as they were allowing costs to mount up, unchallenged. So part of the deal we struck with Ron Dixon was an agreement to sort out Derek's position which we did by giving him a seat on the board and so much of his settlement in shares. Although this also went sour later on and now the board is Peter, myself, Jim Connor and my lawyer Richie Robertson, with Jim as the only paid employee.

'It was always something of a dream for us to be involved with the club and at one point, when they were facing serious VAT problems, I got a call from Malcolm Reid to see if we could help out by buying some property from the club. We were not particularly interested in buying a car park (Densfield Works) but we did, and actually handed over the money before missives were signed. So then we considered just running the club for Dixon, but he insisted on a sale and not only wanted crazy money, he called a press conference to announce the deal before we had agreed. This led to the story of Malcom Reid and Jim Duffy being potential buyers.

'At the beginning, Dundee took up a lot of our time and our other businesses suffered but we have people in place now. I do one full day during the week and another on match days and Peter maintains daily contact. As far as dealings with the players are concerned, I really see them as mercenaries nowadays. Dundee Football Club's a job to them whereas to Peter, me and the supporters – it's in our hearts. The commitment from Ivano and Dario has been excellent and while in the past managers were not very communicative and seemed to be insulted if we asked questions, Ivano and Dario are more open and will answer anything we want. I remember once, after we lost a game, Ivano specifically asked for a meeting with Peter and me so he could explain what had gone wrong. He came down to Peter's house on the Saturday night and spent an hour or two going over the video and his charts, showing what he was trying to do and how players had not always done what had been asked of them. I think it would have been great to have seen him as a player ten years ago.

'We're three or four years into it now and, commercially, it's night and day. I think the new profile has helped the club, the town and Scottish football in general. The Caniggia business was handled satisfactorily by all parties but we're not a bottomless pit – we've made it clear that we will have to sell on a regular basis to balance the books. Our investment is only going to be clawed back on the sale of players. We're still a bit behind but we'd be happy if Dundee could simply break even every year and it may come in a couple of years. We're lucky in that if someone is to be sold, Ivano's contacts mean that someone else is lined up to come in.

'We're also happy with the Scottish players. It was a big thing to get Kenny Cameron on board – 22 years with Dundee United and responsible for a lot of their talent coming through – and Ivano feels that there's definitely room for the Scottish laddies. Recently one of our young boys was set to go to Aberdeen and no one could change his mind. But an hour with Ivano and he decided to stay at Dens. And I think Ivano will definitely see out his own contract. He enjoys the city and his relations with us and, like us, he feels he has a lot to achieve. He sees Dundee as a good platform and we're agreed on the plan. It's a learning process for everybody but the team spirit is there – we saw that on the trip to Belgrade – and I think things will tighten up this season. I'm really looking forward to it.

'Everybody asks where the money comes from, but there's no secret – we have to subsidise things from our other companies, such as the sale of the Mardi Gras. We've paid off a lot of things now, although Peter and I are still at the bottom of the list for getting money back. But the hardest thing is the financial side. If I hadn't put my money into Dundee I probably could have retired or at least had a year off. It takes up a lot of your life and I have a young family. Before one of the games we were walking down to Tannadice and the abuse that we got from the United fans was not very nice. The strange thing is that the two sets of fans are fine when they meet up after the game and at least we're spared sectarianism, which is good.

'I would say that Peter's appetite for football itself is greater than mine. Sometimes, when his heart rules his head, he has to be reined in a wee bit. I think he'll still be keen when he comes back from Spain. When we came in first, we spoke to Jim McLean about ground-sharing because we knew we had to spend all the money on the stands but he would only consider amalgamation, and as Dundee United. With the new Euro 2008 meetings going well, this may change. Dundee Council are up for it, as well as the Scottish Parliament and the SET, so it's down to funding, but it's all positive stuff and the will is there now for it to happen.'

THIRTEEN

KENNY CAMERON:
YOUTH DEVELOPMENT CO-ORDINATOR

BONETTI'S BLUES

These players can just about pass any team to death!

'I'm originally from Perth and an uncle, Alex Cameron, played for Brechin and Forfar but that was my only footballing connection – although my sons play. One is an apprentice professional at Dens, and my daughter also works for the club. I was born in 1942 and just came through the ranks of Boys' Brigade football, played juvenile with Burghmuir Rovers, junior with Perth Celtic and then went to Blairgowrie Juniors. I came to Dundee in 1961 and Bob Shankly signed me after a trial match against United where I scored three goals. I was working in a bank, but wanted to be a professional footballer and signed a provisional form. I finished the season with Blairgowrie then was called up for season 1962–63. I've been more or less full time in football ever since.

'Shankly was brilliant. He was a disciplinarian who kept things simple, and was very honest with his players. At that time it was the fact that Dundee had good players that counted. Tactics weren't so important. Shankly knew what he was doing. I got a few games in my first season. He would give you a few, a taste of the first team, and bring you on gradually. He was forward-thinking, and I learned a lot on the man-management side. He would tell you things to your face. He moved me around a bit too. I played on the left wing for a while.

'The Dundee team was something special and Gilzean was the best finisher I ever saw. And later, there was Charlie Cooke . . . he would be happy in the current team, the Nemsadze role. I can remember a move at Parkhead where Hamilton found Seith, he played the ball in front of Gordon Smith, a pinpoint cross, and Gilzean scored from the penalty spot. It was simple, but the standard of play was unbelievable. All the play was forward. And the game today, with wing-backs getting forward – Hamilton was doing that at that time. Looking back, although I was only involved in a squad sense, it was the best time of my career: very exciting, and later I had some European action myself against Zaragoza.

'Gilzean and Ure moved on, but there were still good players and I scored a lot of goals over the next two or three seasons [including a fantastic strike against Rangers in the 1964 Cup final]. We were still a confident side and I had six or seven seasons. I played for Bobby Ancell, who was a very nice guy, but without the ruthless streak that Shankly had. Then I seemed to lose my way a bit. I moved to Kilmarnock where Malcolm MacDonald was manager. They had also won the League fairly recently (in 1965). I was just married and travelled down with Frank Beattie. They still had some good players there. Jackie McInally, Gerry Queen, McIlroy were there in 1968–69 – but the travelling got to me and I came back to Dundee United.

'I had played briefly for Dundee at the same time as Jim McLean and he made a good impression on me, even at that time. This was the time of players like Alec Kinninmonth, Alec Bryce, wee Billy Campbell and Ally Donaldson. Ancell was trying to turn things around from Shankly's time but, when I think about it, I really learned everything I know about the game from McLean. He coached at Dens then came to Tannadice as manager when I was just reaching that stage in my career when I wasn't so sharp. I was helping the reserve team and Jim asked me to stay on and help with the coaching but I had the chance to go to Montrose with Alex Stuart and I wanted a fresh start. I played, coached and managed there for four years then Jim asked me to go back to Tannadice as chief scout. He was always so knowledgeable and open. He'd say "I need a midfield player: Paul McStay'll do." He set his standards high. I would travel with the first team and his team talks contained ideas that I had never thought about, although he also wanted the opinions of others. "Should I play Dailly up front to give us secure possession?" he'd say. I have total respect for the man. Once he trusted you, he left you to it. So I had a brilliant 12 or 13 years – bringing young players through like Gallacher,

McKinlay, Ferguson, Dailly and Clelland. I had to rely on all the scouts though and we had centres throughout the country.

'I also worked closely with Walter Smith, travelling all over the country, watching matches every night. Walter is a very shrewd man, another excellent man-manager. Once young players were seen to get a chance, it encouraged others. Duncan Ferguson came from a village outside Stirling (Fallin) and signed when he was 13. He was like a young antelope, all arms and legs and didn't play much at first because he was growing and couldn't really run. After the Youth Cup win (he was only a sub) he was in the first team for just a short while before he was away for £4 million. I learned you have to be really patient with young players. Physically, mentally and technically.

'I met Peter Marr four or five years ago, through Paul Sturrock. They were running St Joseph's Juniors and were looking for a coach/manager. Things were not so good at Tannadice and Peter's enthusiasm rubbed off on me. The job wasn't full time (I was doing some sports coaching and development work at Dundee College, still am). I've never regretted the move. It was a fresh challenge and the club did well. Peter always looked for a good team spirit. There was nothing said as far as I was concerned, about the move to Dundee. I just got on with my job at St Joseph's. But Peter eventually asked me to go in, in charge of the youth development. And Jim McLean has always been supportive, a good friend.

'When the Bonettis arrived, things were very different. The normal routine changed, but I had been through similar changes with Ivan Golac and you soon get used to things. It's great, there are fresh ideas, and I think that what they are doing is excellent. There was obviously a bedding-in time but now communications are much better. They bring a different type of tactical knowledge. How to keep the ball press the ball in certain areas. I'm impressed – these players can just about pass any team to death! And now the younger boys, like Boylan and Robb are beginning to come through. Ray Farningham and Stevie Campbell take them on a daily basis and I focus on the younger talent – ages 12 to 16 – with games on a Sunday. I've decided to concentrate on local boys, from Dundee Angus, Tayside and Fife, and I'm really confident that we're going to see players come through. I would just love to see them go all the way.'

FOURTEEN

SEASON 2001–02 (PART ONE)

BONETTI'S BLUES

It is difficult to know what to expect from the new season. Europe is still the target but any improvement would be welcome, and my impression is that, at some point, when Ivano gets the full squad in place that he wants, there will be a big leap. I don't think that the time is just yet and it may be that the lack of close-season break and Inter-Toto effort will take their toll sometime during the season.

The first match of the new season is United versus Dundee and there is virtually a full house for the game, played in warm, windy weather. Tannadice looks compact and modern and there is a great sense of anticipation, although the fixture always seems to bring out an incredible amount of vitriol between the fans. In front of me sit a hippy/fashionable young couple and I reflect upon how I would be reluctant to go into this bearpit with a woman. Just to remind me, someone sitting next to the couple gets arrested for leaping over the wall when a goal is scored. A friend once said to me, 'So why is it acceptable for you to go alone?'

There is a minute's silence for United's great servant Dennis Gillespie who died in the close season, and the teams are on expected lines, with United going for youthful Scottish commitment and Dundee fine-tuning their basic formation in an attempt to put right last season's problems. Langfield is now established as first-choice goalkeeper, Walter Del Rio is paired with Zurab in central defence and Milne lines up with Sara in the attack as Caballero is suspended. Romano is preferred to Artero, who is said to have a gum infection.

The team comprises: Langfield, Smith, Zurab, Del Rio, Marrocco, Romano, Nemsadze, Rae, Carranza, Sara, Milne.

The game starts brightly, with Marrocco showing good skill and attacking flair but there is early difficulty when Langfield brings McIntyre down in the box. Charlie Miller misses the resultant penalty but makes amends a few minutes later when the cultured Partridge swings a good ball into the box and McIntyre gets a touch on. Undeterred, Langfield sends virtually his next clearance the length of the park and Sara pounces to drill in an excellent goal. Dundee proceed to control the match before and after half-time. The central defenders look fairly comfortable, Nemsadze is a constant threat and Rae and Milne are coming more into the game. In 56 minutes Romano plays a great long ball into the box and Sara's knockdown is tapped in by Rae. The tempo of the game immediately rises, with United throwing everyone forward and Dundee having a few scares. They look to have weathered the storm when, deep in injury time, that old, last-minute central-defensive bogey strikes again. A United corner from the right is met by two (virtually unchallenged) United players and ex-Dundee forward Jim Hamilton heads in the equaliser with almost the last touch of the ball. Both managers appear to think it a fair result.

My own feeling is that Zurab and Langfield need bigger physical support and that Wilkie (no relation) would be worth an extended try. In fairness, Bonetti is said to be looking to sign an Argentinian stopper, Luis Medero, for this very reason and, within days, Wilkie is out on loan to Jocky Scott's Notts County. I also feel that, like Del Rio (and Garrido), Romano is technically an excellent player but Artero has the ability to make a telling break and hope that both players' skills will continue to be utilised on the right-hand side.

One final depressing note on the match is the behaviour of young (and not so young) Dundee vandals who can be seen trying to damage the Shed seats at the final whistle. Another good reason for ground-sharing.

On Tuesday, 31 July, both Dundee clubs come together with the local enterprise company and city council to announce their bid for a new (joint) stadium for Euro 2008. United's statement is perhaps the most reserved of those made (with echoes of the oft-repeated Jim McLean position) but the artist's impression is there and a number of Kingsway sites are proposed. The idea is for a ground of 20,000 capacity, which can be increased to 30,000 for the Euro matches, then reduced again, with the space being utilised for local sporting and social facilities. The money (a reported £20–£30 million) is to be found through public/private partnership.

Just before the game with Hibs comes shocking news from Dens. Artero's absence is not down to an infection but to a far more worrying set of symptoms. He has been suffering double vision and poor balance, has been tested for multiple sclerosis and has been returned to Spain to await the results. Javier is only recently married and although nothing is as yet confirmed, this almost feels like a loss in the family to me. I am sure that other fans feel the same way, such is their close identification with these players.

The game is given some extra spice as Hibs' front players are the former United forward Craig Brewster and the Spaniard Francisco Luna who, two seasons previously, was signed to Dundee by Peter Marr along with Artero without the knowledge of Jocky Scott. In a splendid gesture, Carranza wears the Artero strip under his own and the team responds magnificently, with a 2–1 win – a highly significant result given last year's defeats by the Easter Road side. Sara gives Dundee the lead with a clever header and when that goal is equalised in the second half by John O'Neill, Caballero (back in the team for Milne) demonstrates some of his old skills to wrong-foot the last line of defence and win the game for the Dark Blues. Del Rio holds his place alongside Zurab and, the following week, Bonetti tries to bring in a replacement for Artero, the former Reggiano, Bologna and Genoa midfielder, Dario Morello, who played for the out-of-contract Italian side Equipe Romagna against Dundee on their pre-season Italian tour. Thirty-two-year-old Morello is also a former teammate of Ivano's at Genoa. The manager has another appointment with the SFA. With Dario still in the stand following a transgression with Ally McCoist during the last Kilmarnock game and himself chastised for throwing his jacket into the crowd at Parkhead, Ivano now must accompany Peter Marr and Jim Connor to Hampden to contest the employment claims of Patrizio Billio and Marco de Marchi. The SFA decision is split, finding in favour of the club on some counts and the players on others. Dundee withdraw to consider their next move and later decide to appeal.

Sectarianism/Hooliganism

If I happen to wear a green shirt to work and it draws comment I know I am in Glasgow and, although it's usually just fun or even a sartorial compliment, it slightly disappoints me. Thankfully, Dundee, for all its problems and religious and cultural divisions, never seemed to get properly hooked on that one.

I know that there is an undercurrent of this at Dens, but I would not call it full-blown sectarianism (or worse, BNP rubbish). The song line 'the Dundee *Derry* boys', for example, is of comparatively recent origin. It did not exist when the '60s team was winning the League ('the Dundee boys' seemed to suffice) and, from memory, I think it began to appear in the late '60s or '70s, when the team was not doing so well and small gangs of youths were able to make their voices heard as Dundee crowds diminished and Celtic/Rangers rivalry intensified. Of course, given the new cosmopolitan team, none of it makes any sense anyway and, personally, I go for 'Ivano . . . Dario' every time. In fact, I'd like to hear some opera on CD or maybe some rousing Spanish stuff like the Gypsy Kings as the teams come out. Now that *would* make people pay attention to Dundee Football Club and give the fans some new tunes for their own repertoire.

I have written before that neither Dundee nor United, nor even Dundee Hibs, were ever sectarian in their choice of players and it cannot be said often enough. I was once in the company of Eric Milligan, Lord Provost of Edinburgh, well-known Hearts fan and decent man. He had recently been interviewed in one of the Scottish broadsheets and, when asked about sectarianism at Tynecastle, had replied that, whilst not condoning it, it was a fact of life in Scottish football which historically underpinned the game in Glasgow, Edinburgh and Dundee. Not so, I politely informed him, and offered the Dundee facts.

He fixed me with a beady eye and, in that certainty beloved of politicians everywhere, said, 'I can assure you . . . if you are a Catholic from Lochee, you will support Dundee United.' I wonder what he makes of the Marr family and, of course, I can give many more personal examples. For what it's worth, I once had to have the same discussion with another fine fellow – Phil Differ, producer of BBC Scotland's *Only an Excuse* and a Celtic fan. You can see that the issue is confused.

And no one is safe. Even the legendary League-winning skipper who, it is sometimes said, was named after the Bobby Cox Stand, has had to face this strange music. 'My wife comes from Lochee and when we were courting I was in Lochee all the time,' he says, 'yet Celtic fans would shout, "Away ye bluenose, freemason bastard."' Cox, of course, was raised and educated in Dundee as a Catholic.

FIFTEEN

JIM CONNOR:
DIRECTOR AND COMMERCIAL MANAGER

BONETTI'S BLUES

'It was not pulled out of thin air . . .'

Jim Connor was born in 1958 and raised in Longforgan. If not destined to be a sportsman himself, he was 'guaranteed' some kind of sporting role as his father was head groundsman at Dundee High School's sports ground for 27 years. Significantly, like Peter Marr, he has a long pedigree of sports administration and commercial management and, as a former commercial manager for Dundee United, has a comprehensive knowledge, not only of the city's clubs but also of the Scottish game in general, and now the global marketplace that is professional football.

'I always loved football but only played to a poor standard, for Longforgan and the schools (Longforgan, Logie, Harris Academy) and so on. Then I managed a few teams, amateurs and works teams and when I went down south to work, I started a team there, in Kettering. My first job was in sports retail as a trainee manager with Lilywhite's at Draffens. We built it up to be a good outlet and it was a very good grounding. I followed both the city teams and I always had a liking for a certain Glasgow team that plays in green and white. I just always liked the way they played.

'Working backwards, before I came to Dundee I was running my own commercial marketing operation – Premier Sports – which produced handbooks for most of the Premier League and First Division teams and we looked after marketing for some of the Angus clubs. Before that I was Commercial Manager at Tannadice for three years and that was when I first made contact with Dundee via Ron Dixon. Dixon came to Tannadice shortly after he arrived in Dundee, offering to buy Jim McLean's shares. He saw amalgamation as the way forward. I did some research on him and he was listed as someone who took on ailing sporting bodies, secured maximum grant aid and sold them on. I didn't really take to him as a person because I didn't feel he could be trusted and he certainly wasn't a football person. And I think Jim McLean quickly shared that view.

'I was introduced to Peter and Jimmy originally via a mutual friend. Davie Young, and worked with them on the St Joseph's project. It was really a hobby to which we brought our football knowledge, if you like, and commercial ideas.

'One of the things that we achieved was this idea of a big family. We blend well as individuals and as business people and that's a great asset. We always felt that we had our own plans and wanted to do things our own way. Peter talked to Dixon about running the club first of all but carrying the Dixon "baggage" really would not have done the club any favours going forward. We wanted to keep our powder dry until we were in a position to move. Peter and Jimmy would buy the club and I would run it, although I don't have any shareholding. I'm obviously in daily contact with both of them.

'When we came in first, we felt it right that John McCormack be given a chance and he was supported to the best of everyone's ability with the resources available. We then began to perceive frailties in the set-up, however, that we thought would be exposed. Nothing is harder than having to tell somebody they no longer have a job, but we all believed we were doing things for the right reasons and it was soon after that we mapped out the next stage. The same thing applied when Jocky's contract wasn't renewed – we had countless conversations with him – but there are a lot of things to be taken into account when you are running a football club. We were enjoying an upward trend in season ticket sales and we wanted to see that continue.

'I was introduced to Dario Magri through a Yugoslavian agent called Voia Novakcovic and he brought Dario up to Dundee with Patrizio Billio and Walter Del Rio who were both at Crystal Palace. We watched them in a reserve match at Tannadice and I thought both were outstanding, but Jocky wouldn't wear Walter, although he didn't give Victor Ferraz a touch of the ball. I continued to talk to Dario – there was something impressive about him although, on the face of things, he was simply a friend to Italian players in the

English game, and he did a co-ordinating job at Crystal Palace under Lombardo. He was incredibly well connected.

'Dundee were going on a winter break to Cyprus. I suggested that it would be a good idea to bring Dario along and during that week we opened up to one another. He began to talk about Ivano and Dario Bonetti, suggesting that they might play and also invest in the club. We invited Ivano to a derby match and, again, I had done my homework on him. His pedigree was outstanding as a player but the idea of management emerged later.

'Peter and I had been looking at Real Mallorca and other examples of international networking and when we compared our business plan with what Ivano had planned to do in management, we thought we had something exciting. Not many people paid attention at first, but they are doing now. It was not pulled out of thin air. If we had not had the balls to go for it, there is no question that someone else would have, probably in England.

'It shouldn't be forgotten that one of our guiding principles about running a football club is that it should be run at a profit. It was time to make a big decision and we asked Jocky for his ideas. We also spoke to Berndt Schuster and another highly recommended candidate, the French Under-21 national team coach, but fair and square, Ivano had worked on his ideas for some time and presented the best case.'

Right on cue, Steve Archibald arrives in Connor's office and Walter Smith is also expected, from Everton, possibly to run the rule over Gavin Rae. I am reminded of Connor's earlier assertion that Dundee's intentions are serious and that others are taking them seriously.

Connor continues: 'Football clubs are known for a few things, and one of them is losing money. We would hope to eventually buck that trend, although, after showing a small profit in year one, we made a loss last year and will probably do so again this year. However, it is not scaring us because what we have done in effect is raise the value of the club substantially. When we arrived, the value of the Dundee players was something like £1 million. I work very closely with a guy called Bill Gerard, who is a university professor in England and an expert in football business. One of the things he does is impartially value players (Leeds United, for example, will not buy a player without his valuation) and our current figure is now sitting at something nearer £15 million. Ivano may think a bit more, but this is a useful outside opinion, recognised by finance houses – although, curiously, Celtic and Rangers apparently use different benchmarks. Our turnover-to-wage ratio has slipped a bit recently, although the turnover is still increasing at a rapid rate – £700,000 when we arrived, maybe in excess of £4 million this year.

'Ivano is a like-minded person to ourselves. He sees the benefit of sourcing players at little or no cost, developing them and, hopefully, selling them on at a profit. It's all about contacts. We are not dealing with agents so much at the moment – in the main we try to deal direct with players. We are continually dealing with contacts on the telephone: the Bonettis, Dario Magri, Peter Marr, his son Paul (who is now Football Director with the club at Ivano's request, dealing with the players' needs), and myself.

'We also discussed the playing side in some depth – how we all wanted it to be played. Ivano didn't really name names at first, he talked rather about the quality of player he wanted, how he would build the play from the back and so on. While the press were initially contemptuous, we knew that something was about to happen which would change people's minds.

'Ivano is a clever man with a business brain and one of the things important to him – because he has seen it at successful clubs – is the link between the boardroom and playing staff. It has to be exact yet spontaneous. The whole thing has got to work as a unit with no artificial separation. We have heads of departments who meet on a regular basis and everything has to link. There is also a whole range of systems now in place, for housing, doctors etc.

'When we talked about the quality of player who was coming

into the club, we had to have budgets and Ivano has done well on that score. But a player like Caniggia simply would not have talked to us in the past, whether we could have afforded him or not. We had confidence in Ivano and Dario as they had played for some of the best coaches in the world and the fact that one is the forward player and the other is a defender works well in this area. But we knew it would take some time.'

SIXTEEN

SEASON 2001–02 (PART TWO)

BONETTI'S BLUES

A crowd of around 8,000 welcomes Premier League newcomers Livingston to Dens for the third match of the season. Both teams have four points, Livingston having beaten Hearts and drawn with Rangers. The management team of Jim Leishman and David Hay have their own contingent of foreign players, among whom some former Steve Archibald/Airdrie players are prominent. The forward Fernandez looks particularly useful and the cuddly Leishman warmly embraces Ivano before the match. I also notice that one of the young Dundee mascots still has Caniggia on his shirt – gone but never to be forgotten. It is a scrappy game, but one in which Sara once again proves his worth, deftly heading in his third goal in three matches, and from another pinpoint Romano cross. In fairness, Livingston are unlucky not to equalise. Bingham chips Langfield beautifully in the first half only to see the shot come off the bar and the Dundee goalkeeper makes a couple of great saves in the second half. Zurab and Del Rio are otherwise competent, Carranza, Rae and Nemsadze all have their moments and Caballero, although drawing a lot of flak from the terraces for going it alone, is always purposeful and unorthodox, which makes him a handful for defences. Marrocco is carried off with what looks like a bad knee injury and I am impressed by the fact that Dario Bonetti immediately leaves his seat in the stand to check on the full-back's condition. Marcello is well covered by Garrido and, that night, Dundee sit third in the League, two points behind Celtic and equal on points with Rangers. It is the first time the Bonettis have won two consecutive home games and this is surely another step in the right direction. I am slightly uneasy about the fact that Livingston appear to have had more appetite for the game but cheered once again by substitute Stephen Milne's eagerness and continuing progress.

The following week reveals that neither Medero nor Morello will be coming to Dens and, given Marrocco's injury, it is a peculiar re-shuffle (not unlike the last Tynecastle line-up) which faces Hearts at Tynecastle. Romano mysteriously moves from a right-forward to a left-back position, with Garrido going into the left midfield and Carranza swapping over. Another large travelling support is delighted by the new, Argentine-style away strip but is horrified to see the game going almost exactly the same way as the last two League encounters. Following ten minutes or so of Dundee composure, Hearts appear to raise the tempo (and physical stakes) and, within a five-minute spell, Dundee are three goals down. Cameron (who has done this repeatedly to Dundee) darts into space to convert a Fulton free kick; Nemsadze and the defence stop for a handball which is not given, and Wales is free to score with a good shot. Then there is the usual, defensive failure as the Maroons charge in for a cross ball, McKenna is unchecked on the left and a touch into the box gives Wales his second. What the fans are supposed to make of this is anybody's guess but they remain good humoured, even if the players do not. Del Rio, in particular, is lucky to stay on the pitch when he knees Juanjo in the backside following a hard tackle. The incident leads to a mini brawl and I can't help feeling that Bonetti may now mark the Argentinian's card for a place in the youth squad with Billio and de Marchi. Del Rio is actually playing well but the manager remains stuck for a defender, or someone who will provide tenacity and leadership.

The team plays some good football in the second half but Sara is repeatedly caught offside and, although there is a brilliant solo goal near the end from Nemsadze, it cannot disguise the Dundee frustration. Hearts win the game 3–1. Ivano's post-mortem is interesting, as usual. It will be the last time this happens at Tynecastle, says the Dundee boss, as the Dark Blues play better football and generally have more quality than their opponents.

Ibrox

I have been to Ibrox many times but took a decision in 1987 that I wasn't going to go back. It was the game in which Jim Duffy injured his knee and, as it was the only area we could get a ticket for, myself and a friend were standing among the Rangers support underneath the main stand. I had a new book out and, as we took our places, my friend said, 'How is the book going?' Before I could answer, a Rangers fan with a moustache turned round and said, 'Are you an author?'

'No, no,' I said, without any false modesty, but before I could explain, the man says, 'Because I am. Who is your publisher? Perhaps he would publish my book?'

With that, he thrusts a business card into my hand and I put it in my pocket, mumbling that I will see what I can do and pointedly watching the game. After some minutes he turns around again. I have noticed he is wearing a large hand-knitted Rangers scarf. 'Do you read *Life and Work?*' he asks. (*Life and Work* is the magazine of the Church of Scotland.)

'No,' I reply, with a smile.

'What's funny about that?' he demands.

'Nothing,' I say, 'I'm just here to watch the match.' He turns back and goes silent for a while. Suddenly, he turns to me again, obviously angry.

'Right . . . don't do anything for me,' he says, with a Donald Findlay slant of the eyes. 'We have nothing in common and [raising his voice] DUNDEE SUPPORTERS SHOULD NOT BE IN THIS PART OF THE GROUND!'

My mate and I look at one another in disbelief. My mate stands around six feet four, so I am relatively fearless, but I have been in company at Ibrox which has been hit by cans and hot pies, and attacked in the Broomloan Stand toilets before proper segregation was introduced. Things are not bad here, but they could be. 'Fortunately', Dundee lose, but we're still shocked by the man's irresponsible behaviour.

Later, in the car, my pal says, 'What was that guy's problem?'

'God knows, but he gave me his card.' I reach into my pocket. It says he is The Reverend somebody or other, a Batchelor of Divinity.

SEVENTEEN

SEASON 2001–02 (PART THREE)

BONETTI'S BLUES

This week I am swithering about going to Ibrox partly because I feel Dundee can take something from the game and partly through Caniggia curiosity. It is, however, uncertain whether my former hero will play and we have a family event at home so I elect to listen to the radio then watch it on TV. Dundee fans can be heard singing throughout much of the game (big change there) and the Dens Park Dynamo dominates the early stages before Rangers score with a Mols goal which is reminiscent of Caballero's at Parkhead. Sara misses a couple of pretty clear headed chances and the pundits question his bravery, but not Ivano, who later praises the same quality in his striker. One thing which amuses me is Gordon Smith of Radio Scotland reflecting upon what a Dundee fan who had been abroad for a few years would make of the scene: 'His team full of continentals, wearing the Argentine strip and – let's face it – dominating large parts of the game with much better players than Rangers.'

'But can they score?' asks Murdo MacLeod at half-time. 'I feel as though the tools go down once a goal is scored against them.'

'Rubbish,' says the indefatigable Chick Young, once a critic, now a convert to the Bonetti cause. 'I could watch this team all day.'

'Then you're as well to watch them in training,' says MacLeod, combatively. 'Something stops them winning as often as they should. This is possibly the best side technically in Scottish football, but there is vulnerability.'

In the second half, Langfield loses a very poor second goal and ex-Dundee player Neil McCann is sent off for a shocking, two-footed tackle on Barry Smith. This gives the Dundee fans some hope but, for the second week running, Beto does something 'stupit' and this time receives a red card. Dundee are back in sixth spot, although not before Ivano offers the press one of his frank post-match assessments. Rangers, he says, have no chance of winning the League, Dundee had 70 minutes of the game, and only three Rangers players – Claudio, Latapy and Amoruso – would get a game in the current Dark Blues' side. This, you can imagine, goes down a bundle with the west coast press. *The Scotsman's* Alan Pattullo is slightly more phlegmatic: 'I don't recall a Dundee manager ever having said that before,' he says.

There is more drama off the field. Wolves (having signed Colin Cameron from Hearts) enquire about Caballero but are put off by the price tag, and then Artero issues an open letter to the fans to tell them that muscular sclerosis has indeed been diagnosed. This is very sad for a great player who is recently married, but he also says the prognosis is good and that he hopes to be playing again soon.

Dundee versus St Johnstone is a game that the Dark Blues simply must win and a very creditable crowd of more than 7,000 turns out to see them do it. There is an unfortunate statistic that Dundee have not won this fixture at Dens in the Premier League since 1983 but Saints have only one point and should really be there for the taking. Although the media says Dundee will be at full strength, Sara is on the bench and Garrido comes in for Carranza, who is suspended. Gavin Rae has the ball in the net right away before being judged offside, then young Milne makes his mark getting on to the end of a good Caballero cross to score in three minutes. The familiar pattern of failure to consolidate the win sets in, however, and Dundee have one or two near things, as Del Rio makes a goal-line save from Parker and Dasovic hits the bar with Langfield beaten. I reflect that Dasovic might be the kind of aggressive, driving midfielder that Dundee need, although Rae is also playing well and has one or two useful long-range attempts. Both Zurab and Nemsadze, who have had midweek international duties with Georgia, look sluggish. Dundee start the second half with more purpose but cannot score, and when Saints substitute MacDonald is brought down in a relatively harmless position at the corner of the box by Smith, we fear the worst. Darren Jackson converts the penalty and the fans slope off. Peter Marr is present for the game and if I were he, I would be having a word with Ivano before returning to Spain. When or how are we going to find the steel, the ruthlessness, to finish off the good build-up?

EIGHTEEN

BONETTI'S SCOTS

It is generally accepted that if the Bonetti experiment is to succeed, it must include a number of Scottish players. Not necessarily immediately, but young local players must be brought through if the team is to retain local support and the 'foreign mercenaries' tag rebutted. There are also implications for the Scottish game in general and the international team.

Initially, the side contained goalkeeper Robert Douglas (now the Celtic number one), central defender Steven Tweed (since transferred), midfielder Gavin Rae (now a Scotland cap) and right-back/sweeper Barry Smith, who was first made club captain by John McCormack and who has retained the position under Ivano. Although, in Craig Brown's words the Italians 'might not be able to make a continental player of him', the Dundee manager speaks very highly of Barry's commitment and leadership qualities and gave him a new contract.

Beyond this, there are young first-team (or squad) players like Langfield and Milne, as well as Boylan, MacKay and Forbes, who have made a number of first-team appearances in the 2001–02 season, and also Souter, the young reserve goalkeeper. The encouraging thing from my point of view is the calibre of youth and schoolboy coaches which the club has employed and the faith that these individuals have in the next generation of Dundee FC and Scottish talent.

Barry Smith
Dundee FC

'I was born in Paisley in 1974. My family's team was always St Mirren and I followed then as a youngster. My father played as a junior for Ayrshire teams – Maybole and Beith – and, on my mother's side, two uncles played for Bolton. I have one sister and one brother who also played football and had the chance to go senior with Morton, but he chose to go to university.

'I started with St Mary's Primary in Paisley and then St Andrews

Secondary. My brother played for Renfrew Waverley and, although their youngest team was Under-10, I was playing for them when I was eight. Renfrew then became St Mirren Boys Club, who I played for for a couple of seasons, then I played for Barrhead for four seasons and finally Celtic Boys Club (Under-16) which was run by Frank Cairney.

'I signed S-form for Celtic on an Easter Monday and, on the Tuesday back at school, St Mirren came up with the same offer. Had the clubs come in the other way round, I probably would have signed for Saints, because I was a supporter.

'Barry Lavety and Barry McLaughlin played in the district team with me – it was Tony Fitzpatrick's time at St Mirren – and one of their young stars, Paul Lambert, had played with my brother at Linwood Rangers. I played in the centre of defence or midfield and even as a striker at school. I went straight to full time with Celtic after school in 1991 and I was the only one in my year who made it to the first team although Brian McLaughlin and Brian O'Neill were in the previous year's intake. I was actually signed by Tommy Craig but, once the season started, Liam Brady arrived and I enjoyed playing under him – I thought he had a lot of good ideas.

'I made the first team, in my first year and my debut was against Falkirk [who won 3–4]. The following Wednesday we went to Neuchatel in Switzerland and lost 5–1. I was a sub and playing right-back at the time. There were a lot of good players at Celtic. Big Tony Mowbray was a great influence on me and had a great attitude, and Dziekanowski was the most skilful player I've ever seen – but they were going through a bad spell and I played most of my games towards the end of the seasons, 19 games in all, over four or five seasons.

'By then, Tommy Burns was the manager and I just wasn't in his plans, which is fair enough, but at 21 I thought I should be playing first-team football and when the chance came to move to Dundee I couldn't knock it back. My money also improved.

'I came to Dundee in 1995–96 as part of the deal with Morten

Wieghorst going to Celtic. Jim Duffy was manager and he was always good to me. Every manager has different qualities and he really helped me along as a defender. He was playing centre-half when I signed but, after the half season, we went to three at the back with me as centre-half and himself as sweeper. Then he finished playing and I took his position. The club was very different at that time. There was always something in the paper about it shutting up shop and you didn't know what to expect. Duffy then went to Hibs and had a great start there. I have a lot of time for him, since he gave me my chance.

'John McCormack made me captain, which was a good thing for me, and there were one or two good signings like Rab Douglas and James Grady. Then the Marr family came in but, to be honest, I didn't pay a lot of attention to these things . . . as long as I was paid at the end of the month. There weren't massive changes immediately. We just knew they had a three-year plan, or whatever, to get into the Premier League – and we got up in one.

'The management changes were obviously unexpected, especially when you're top of the League, but players are often going to be at clubs longer than managers, so you just get on with it. If you work hard and show that you're willing to play for that manager, you should be OK. Jocky didn't change things that much. We had been playing good football under Cowboy but that was in the lower division. Things had to change in the Premier but you go to every ground not knowing what's going to happen and, in some ways, that's easier. We finished fifth in our first season, which was great, but there was a lot of pressure put on the defence – myself, big Brian Irvine, Robbie Raeside. The last few games of that season we played four at the back and only lost once in the last eight games.

'When the stories started about Jocky possibly going, Peter and Jimmy [Marr] called me in. They said whatever happened, it was a case of the team just getting on with things. No one knew what to expect with Ivano and Dario. Italy is obviously one of the great footballing nations in recent years but we didn't know what their ideas would be. A Scottish pre-season is hard but the Italians focus more on aerobic fitness, your heart. I didn't find the pre-season so hard, but I have a natural physical fitness and didn't notice much difference during games. But it affects different people in different ways. I had played the last five or six games of the previous season at right-back and that's where Ivano and Dario had seen me. They shaped up the back four and just adjusted our play as we went along. Nothing radically different, but there is a better quality of player and so you get better quality football. It's all about the team and how it gels – play one touch if it's on. The mentality is important; what you eat, when you sleep – they believe that it's what you do before the game that helps your play. Pre-season we would train, eat, sleep then go through it again in the afternoon.

'When the different faces came in I thought "Well, am I going to be here or not?" but after the initial phase it was fine. And Ivano has been very supportive of me. When a new manager comes in, I believe that you give 100 per cent and if it doesn't work out, you know you've done your best.

'We couldn't believe it when Claudio was first suggested for Dundee. He's a great player and is still proving it at Rangers. And, quite apart from football, although he had played in World Cups with Maradona and everything, he came in and was an ordinary guy who would talk to anyone and would help the young strikers.

'As for the future, as long as we progress, as long as we're not static, then anything is possible.'

Gavin Rae

'I'm originally from Aberdeen, was born in 1977, and both sides of the family came from the North-east. My father's family is from Aberdeen and my mother's from Forres. My grandfather played football post-war, but not to a terribly high standard so there was no footballing tradition. The family always followed Aberdeen and, when I was young, they had that great team with Gordon Strachan, Jim Bett, Willie Miller and Alex McLeish. I played at primary school at Glashievan, at the Bridge of Don and, when I was there, I think we won everything that was going. A number of boys went on to senior teams. Derek Wyness [Aberdeen and Caley] is my best mate and Jamie Watt too, who's at Deveronvale now. It was the same at secondary school – a couple of good players came to Dundee, although they didn't make it. I progressed to Aberdeen juvenile select teams. At that age I played mostly at centre-half or in the centre of midfield. I played centre-half for my youth team, so it's a position I can easily play, although centre midfield is definitely my favourite.

'When I was younger and playing for Deeside Boys Club, Rangers watched me a couple of times and I trained with Dundee United in Aberdeen but they didn't follow up. I ended up going to Brechin and played in the Youth Cup for them. I enjoyed it, travelling down a couple of nights a week for training, when I was still at school. It was one level up from where I was in Aberdeen and they asked me to sign, but Dundee came in around the same time [1995] and they were full time, so that was it. Jim Duffy and John McCormack actually came up, watched me and asked me personally to sign, so that made the difference. They invited me down to see the ground and my parents came down too. I was two years YTS at first. In my first year pro, Duffy went away to Hibs at Christmas. He was a brilliant influence, both as a player and coach. I used to love training. It was hard to start with, moving away from Aberdeen, staying in digs, but you get used to it.

'I would play with the youth team and the reserve team on a Monday night. Sometimes I was in the squad for the first team. I struggled in the first year of YTS, not really making any impression, but when they asked me to come again for a second year, it gave me a bit of confidence. My parents were also very supportive. I was at the end of my fifth year when I was asked to sign. I was supposed to be doing Highers, so they were a bit disappointed, but

I felt I just had to take the chance and they have backed me all the way since then. I suppose, otherwise, I would have done something with computers.

'At the end of my second YTS year, I managed to get five games in the first team, in the First Division. It was the year Dunfermline went up. Dundee had had some good players since the time I arrived: big Morten Wieghorst – his skill and dedication, plus his attitude off the park, everything was first class; and Neil McCann was there; excellent player.

'When Duffy went and John got the job, nothing much changed. I was in and out the team, but still young and still learning. When the Marrs came in, however, he had a bit more money to spend and I didn't figure in the team. It was hard because that was the season I thought I would break through and the manager brought in more experienced players like Jim McInally. I only played one game in the championship season and that still hurts because I didn't get a championship medal and I was one of the longest-serving players here. Jocky had taken over by then and I saw it as a fresh start. We played a couple of reserve matches where he wanted to see all the boys he wasn't familiar with and I did well in these games. It gave me my confidence back and Jocky praised me to the reserve team coach, Ray Farningham.

'I played the last game of the season [1997–98] and the start of the next season, at central midfield. Jim McInally was there and, with so much experience, he made things easier. He would put me right about positional play; when to stay and when to move. I played 23 games in total and we finished very strongly. I had a run of 13 or 14 games at the end of the season, so that helped and the season after I played every game.

'It was disappointing when Jocky left because he was so good to me and my career had changed for the better. I was 21 and going to Ibrox and Parkhead, playing every week, it was excellent. Anyway, Ivano came to meet the players at 7.30 on a Friday night – quite a strange time, before Saturday training, and training itself changed dramatically. Pre-season had been total running solid, for two weeks, really hard. With Ivano you would run in the morning and the afternoon would be ball-work. It was still hard, but spaced out and not so intense. There were more hours in the course of the day. When he came first, though, I was out of the team again, which was obviously disappointing.

'He had said he would stick with me but I was getting agitated and he asked me to bide my time. Eventually, one of the boys was sent off at Hibs and I got a chance against St Mirren. I played well and, against Montrose in the CIS Cup, I got man of the match. On the Saturday though, there was a new signing in and I wasn't even on the bench! I was in the Stand. That was no use. So I went to see Ivano and my agent and asked to get away if I wasn't going to be playing every week. Again, he said he believed in me and told me to be patient, so I was and when I got back in the team I stayed there.

'We have the players to do certain jobs. He has brought in such good players, he doesn't expect me to battle so much, going forward. He wanted me to discipline myself a lot more, play in central midfield, get the ball and pass it. If you get a chance to go forward, he says, fair enough. If you don't, don't worry. Just stay. And it's good, I'm enjoying it.

'Georgi Nemsadze, just as an example, is such a good player to play with as, of course, is Claudio. I couldn't believe it when he walked through the door. We had seen a lot of good players come to Dens but Claudio – you just couldn't believe it. Everything about his game is special. He's a world star, yet he was prepared to come here and try his best.

'And now the Scotland thing has happened for me. There was a double-header, Belgium, the 2–2 game which I wasn't picked for, but a couple of guys got injured and I was called up for the San Marino game. I was on the bench and obviously delighted. Then I was in the squad against Poland and played the whole game. It was great experience and, again, there were some great players: Don

Hutchison, and Paul Lambert, whose style I really like to learn from.

'There has been some transfer speculation and I have an agent but I hardly ever speak to him. Apart from contractual matters, I'm not interested. I take things as they come and I'm more than happy with Dundee at the moment.'

NINETEEN

SEASON 2001–02 (PART FOUR)

BONETTI'S BLUES

On 11 September 2001 the world is shocked by a horrifyingly audacious piece of international terrorism. Literally out of a clear blue sky two hijacked passenger aircraft are flown straight into the twin towers of the landmark World Trade Center in New York. Another dive-bombs the Pentagon and a fourth crashes on its way to Camp David. The New York incident kills around 7,000 people and the west goes into mourning. Ivano calls for a postponement of the Premier card, but his appears to be a lone voice, and it is a distraught crowd and depleted Dundee team which stands for a minute's silence before the home game with Celtic.

Dundee are without Sara, Caballero and Carranza yet, amazingly, dominate the first half and come close to scoring through both Nemsadze and Robertson before losing a goal to Larsson in the final minute of the forty-five. In the second half, Larsson scores again, as does Petrov with a screamer, before Del Rio is sent off for two yellow cards. The unhappy Dundee afternoon is completed by a fourth goal from Maloney and the Dark Blues slip to ninth in the League. Bonetti is concerned about some of the referee's decisions and offers a memorable quote about Chris Sutton 'looking for a swimming pool' before the free kick which led to the first goal (curiously, Celtic are on the receiving end of a dive in their next match, against Juventus). Ivano continues to face an uphill psychological struggle, given the injury and disciplinary situation and the continuing inability to score or win.

My faith is restored at the next game, against Kilmarnock. The Killie are a good old Scottish club, with a history not unlike our own – provincial status with the occasional domestic trophy and European campaign – although Alex Totten and Bobby Williamson have taken the club to upper-table consistency in recent years. The old ground, situated in a prosperous part of the town off Rugby Road, has given way to a magnificent stadium which enjoys easy access and parking.

The main stand contingent is also not unlike Dundee's (slightly older and perhaps more old-fashioned than some clubs) and they currently enjoy an establishment support from the likes of ex-polisman Sir John Orr and Gordon Jackson MSP.

The atmosphere in certain parts of the ground is therefore often quite couthy, good-humoured and fuelled, no doubt, by the 'famous' Killie pies. This also makes for an appreciation of Dundee's current footballing skills, although the match is a poor one and does not stop one irate fan from managing to squeeze most known Scottish prejudices into one sentence: 'Away an' open a chip shop, ya shower ae effin' gypsy tinks!'

Well, the 'gypsy tinks' today are sadly depleted. There's no Nemsadze, Sara or Del Rio and, after a bright ten minutes, Romano also goes off with a damaged calf. On comes a young player with a famous footballing name, Dave MacKay, who has recently returned from a loan spell with Arbroath. But his arrival coincides with a period of sustained Killie pressure and he looks to be off the pace, before settling into a good game. Marrocco, on the other side, it must be said, is consistently excellent.

Slowly, Dundee's shape begins to improve. It's as though everybody remembers the importance of concentration and, in 38 minutes, the hard-working Garrido fights for a ball on the left-wing. His cross is headed on by Milne and a Robertson lay-off finds Rae who drives a great shot into the net. In the second half, Ivano introduces two new, young Argentinian signings, Gatti and Naveda, and both slot in admirably to assist in the victory. There's one more highlight: a fantastic, leaping take and volley by Caballero which just clears the bar – but, for once, I am fairly confident that the team will see out a victory and not lose something at the death. This is because Langfield is outstanding, Smith assists Zurab in a very safe-looking central defence and the others are moving back and forward with more purpose. All things considered, Ivano's positon is considerably more secure than some, a fact underlined when first Billy Davies and then Sandy Clark lose their management jobs at Motherwell and St Johnstone, respectively, the following week.

BONETTI'S BLUES

I take confidence from this match firstly because the Scots (I include the Aussie Robertson) are doing better; and secondly, the players are generally showing better team play and understanding. I feel that if the specialists – Sara, Caballero and Nemsadze – can hit form, we'll be in third or fourth place by Christmas (famous last words).

The good news continues with a midweek victory at Hamilton in the CIS Cup. Although still missing Nemsadze and Sara, plus Caballero who is suspended, the pattern of the game follows that of Rugby Park: Dundee soaking up some pressure, then scoring with two out of three or four chances. It is a little alarming that Second Division Hamilton have so much of the game, but I take heart from the fact that a number of young, homegrown Scots, including Forbes and Boylan, get a game and do reasonably well. Also, the visiting support at the poetically named Ballast Stadium is around the 1,000 mark, as it was at Kilmarnock.

Unfortunately, the roof falls in the following Saturday at Dens when Aberdeen visit and go away with a 4–1 victory. Although the Dark Blues, inspired by Carranza, have much of each half and score with a lovely goal from Caballero, Langfield (recently included in the Scotland squad with Rae) has a number of problems and the defence/midfield link goes AWOL. Instead of claiming third place, Dundee slip to eighth.

In the following days, the website fans are very critical. 'What kind of team loses four goals to Aberdeen?' 'Jocky's teams never defended so poorly.' 'Discipline is shocking.' And so on. Ivano is also reading the riot act. To make matters worse, Zurab has also been involved in a nasty incident, appearing to have been knocked out by the Aberdeen player Dadi. There are accusations by the African of racist remarks but this is strenuously denied by Dundee and Dadi is eventually fined by the Dons.

Before the next CIS game – which Dundee lose 2–1 to Ross County away – the SFA announce their preferred candidates for Euro 2006 stadium improvement and the Dundee clubs are shortlisted along with Hibs and Aberdeen. The preferred site is the south-west corner of Caird Park at the junction of Kingsway and Aberdeen. Dick Advocaat is quoted as saying that the money should instead go towards improving young Scottish players (in the wake of Scotland's exit from the 2002 World Cup). I tend to think that, given a projected £500 million boost to the Scottish economy, both things are possible and hope for a new Dundee city stadium – the 'San Cairdie'.

On the playing front, the bad news continues with a hapless away defeat (0–1) at East End Park, Dunfermline. The team remains depleted by injury and, in Nemsadze's case, it looks longer term. Ivano is disappointed but philosophical, saying that his young replacement players had performed well. He also announces that better news regarding experienced replacements is on the horizon.

TWENTY

THE FANS

An amazing time in our lives.

Some fans go to extraordinary lengths to watch their team. I remember one, Willie Reilly, telling me that had left his wedding reception with his new wife to see Dundee play Clyde. Dave Forbes, who now runs the Dundee FC Shop, once thought of emigrating but decided against it because he could not face life without the Dark Blues.

Dave Forbes

'I was born in 1942 and can remember Billy Steel coming to Dundee. In fact, one of my pals, Brian Latto, is in the famous picture, pointing to Steel as he runs out to play his first game, and I also did wee jobs at Tannadice in those days. The tannoy used to play "The Jacqueline Waltz" by Will Starr and when it reverberated around the streets on match day, it was like the call for the faithful to come. I would help to put up the nets and lay out the strips. There was steep stairway up to the first floor of the pavilion in the corner and this was effectively the directors' box, above the dressing-rooms. The players around then were Frankie Quinn, Peter MacKay, Johnny Coyle and Jimmy Reid, who still has his wee shop in the Seagate.

'But I was never a United fan. My father was a Dundee fan and I followed him. By the early '60s I had joined the police and their team played at Dens, so I got to know the great players from that era. Charlie Cooke was once needing a lift to the station in a hurry and I took him on the back of my scooter! Charlie has been in touch recently and hopes to visit Dens on his next trip to the UK. He lives in Cincinnati and was genuinely surprised to learn that he is still fondly remembered here. Some great players have been through Dundee's hands and the club has often got the blame, but if players want to go there's nothing you can do.

'I had always watched the team, home and away, for years but I first came to work here when Ron Dixon was chairman. They had grandiose ideas for the centenary year, but folk wouldn't buy tickets because the team wasn't doing well. The best thing was the Sportsman's Dinner where the '60s' team was reunited, just before Hammy died. When the Marrs came, their commitment to the club was well known. I also knew Peter through working with his construction firm; I was a Director of Trojan demolition.

'Dixon had given us a lot of hope but ultimately was out for himself. Angus Cook, on the other hand, would have loved Dundee to have been successful but he seemed to take the flak for the players' shortcomings. The Marrs had better business contacts who could support the club and the changes regarding the Bonettis have been highly successful. No one can doubt that at all. I came to the shop earlier this year and we have seen its turnover rise dramatically. I took last year's shirt stock, put 10 per cent onto it and it sold in nine days. Claudio raised sales, and the Argentinian strip has done it again. If you stay in Dundee, you can see the difference. Five years ago, all you saw was tangerine. It was a surprise to see someone in a Dundee top. Recently, I drove between Claypotts and Dawson Parks and I couldn't believe the number I saw.

'On the park, as far as I'm concerned, we're the best footballing team in the Premier Division. If we could score we would be unbeatable, but the sad fact is we can't get the ball in the net. Even Celtic directors have admitted this to me. Ivano enthuses you, but the lack of goals is a problem, although Caballero is beginning to sharpen up. You even see them on the pitch after the games trying to sort things out. And there's this feeling that the ball players are not being protected – but we've heard that for years.

'Of course there are problems of language and meaning with all the different nationalities as far as the press are concerned, although you do get a laugh! Marianne, Claudio's wife, said to me one day "Beto Carranaza and your wife came to visit me." I say, "No. Beto Carranza and *his* wife. You'll be getting people into trouble!" Claudio and his family still come back regularly to Dundee. He enjoyed his time here and made a lot of friends.

'I like the idea of ground-share but not amalgamation. It would take generations and a great deal of success for one team to get the full support. There are also so many distractions now. In the past I would arrange my holidays so as not to miss a game, but not so much now. Although, if I was on holiday, my mobile would be going right at the end of the match to tell me how the team had done. Recently, a man brought his new-born son to Dens on the day of the child's birth, then back to the hospital.'

I met two further fans for a chat at the Dundee Hilton one Saturday in October 2001.

Robin Grimmond
Founding editor, *Eh mind o' Gillie* fanzine

'I was born in 1954. I come originally from Arbroath and was raised in Kirriemuir. I supported Arbroath until the late '70s but became disillusioned for various non-footballing reasons. They often had good players like Billy Pirie and John Fletcher who went on to other clubs, and they were shafted when the Premier League cut was made. They also never recovered from Albert Henderson's sacking.

'I moved to Dundee in the early '70s to work, and I started going to Dens and Tannadice. I had to make a choice and I actually chose Dundee the year after United won the League because most of my mates were following Dundee, in spite of the relative position of the clubs. I thought there was a passion about the club, and on the terraces as well, and I've never regretted it.

'Dundee were my brother's team and I always remember them as a good footballing side. A lot of folk went to see them from Angus and Fife. I remember going to one game in the season 1961–62. It was 0–0 and Rangers were just playing for the draw. Doug Baillie kicked the ball over the enclosure. But the early '80s side was blood and guts. John McCormack was playing, and a lot of duffers. Then there were some good sides, the John Brown team and the Tommy Coyne/Keith Wright side that just peaked a wee bit early. And in the '90s, Duffy had some excellent young players, although the club was on the verge of closure.'

Ryan 'Paddy' Ireland
Deputy editor, the dundeefc website

'I've lived in Broughty Ferry for 20 years [Ryan was born in 1975] and went to Grove Academy. The earliest time I can remember is the Donald McKay period. My father was, and still is, a huge Dundee fan, going every week. He travelled to Europe with them in the '60s. I still play football for the High Corner [Dundee FC supporters' pub] in the Sunday League.

Ireland – I think we knew it was coming when Cowboy lost his job. We heard at a Stirling Albion match that Jocky was coming in.

Grimmond – We were top of the League, but scraping results and you got the impression that it wouldn't take much for them to be caught. Did McCormack have the know-how to get them up? That was the worry.

Ireland – We knew of the Marrs through the Joeys juniors. They had been putting big money into that set-up and I think people were expecting them to be the next owners, although how much money they had to put in, no one knew.

Grimmond – They were local businessmen but couldn't compete with some of the SPL chairmen.

Ireland – One of the most important things was getting local people back and involved. Obviously someone in Canada could just have shut the club down, whereas if local people are behind it then you know their hearts are in the right place.

Grimmond – They were football people and that was the difference. They knew the game. And it was totally focused because as soon as they won promotion, the team seemed to relax, and it continued into the next season. They were favourites to go down and Alloa put them out of the League Cup.

Ireland – When they got a last-minute penalty against Celtic, when Annand was tripped in the box, things began to improve. They won at Tynecastle and things started to get better, but even then they weren't that far away from the relegation zone.

Grimmond – Jocky's departure was a gradual thing. He wasn't getting his contract renewed and, although they were secure enough in the League, the football was pretty dire.

Ireland – Then Artero and Luna arrived, foisted on him, and there were other players: Barry Elliot, Chris Coyne, Billio – it was clear that Jocky wasn't buying them.

Grimmond – This was the January, February. Dundee fans tend to be split anyway. They were split over Cowboy and split over Scotty. They knew they would survive under Jocky but you could count on one hand the number of entertaining games that season and they got a few cuffings from the Old Firm.

Ireland – They were looking like relegation material until Luna and Artero came in.

Grimmond – When the Bonettis arrived, they had a press conference in the Ferry at the Ballinard Hotel and, to the press, it was just a big joke.

Ireland – It was typical Scottish tabloid mentality – who are these unknowns? And you compare their international standing in the game with that of Bobby Williamson or Sandy Clark. I knew who Ivano was, in the Italian game. I also remembered the Grimsby punching incident – which might have been a bit dodgy – but I had Serie A tapes from Sky games and I got them out immediately. I had one of a Juve game where Ivano and Dario were on the same side and Marco de Marchi was playing for the opposition. I also have Caniggia tapes, against Cameroon.

Grimmond – Yeah, when he goes on a run and gets fouled about four times . . . that's always quoted.

Ireland – It's a fresh mentality. I'm sure I remember Jocky saying you can't compete with Celtic and Rangers but I expect competition and there are teams abroad which have small crowds, like Auxerre, and they compete – they beat the Celtics and Rangers in European competition. Yet the headlines called Ivano and Dario 'Amateurs' because Sestrese contained some amateur players, in Serie C.

So a big support went through for the first Raith Rovers friendly. The word had come through from the Italian training camp, and everyone was really excited. Sara and Caballero had just arrived and, when the team ran out, the hairs went up on the back of my neck. I thought, 'This is something new.'

Grimmond – Even the keepie-uppy was spectacular.

Ireland – Then we went to Grimsby and Nemsadze scored a brilliant goal. He beat about five men. And the support, 2,500, that went through to that first game at Motherwell – someone said it was like a Scottish Cup match.

Grimmond – By the Hibs game, the novelty had worn off and they were now a threat. So that was the start of a press campaign and the referees were lapping it up. As soon as someone went down it was a dive.

Ireland – The away support was fantastic, although I'm not always comfortable with some of the chants.

Grimmond – As far as the Dundee/Derry thing goes, I don't think people believe they are singing something sectarian.

Going through the team now, I think Jamie Langfield might have had more games when he was understudy to Douglas. Robert was getting played with a leg injury and that time would have given Langfield some experience.

Marrocco is a clever player but was better when Bonetti was there to overlap with. Ivano was a great player for us last

year and he's been really missed. Zurab is a class player and
Del Rio is doing better in central defence than at full-back.
But neither is a real centre-half.

Ireland – I think there are two tiers of player. There's Nemsadze,
Caballero, Sara, Carranza and Zurab but Ivano needs a few
more like that.

Grimmond – Sara maybe doesn't always punch his weight but you
realise how good a player he is when he's not there. He's a
great target man and gets into good positions.

Ireland – I'm a bit concerned about Romano, I don't rate him too
highly but I'm concerned that the fans are getting on his
case, when they don't need to.

Grimmond – He's getting played in an attacking wing-back role and
you can't really compare him with Artero, who is a
marvellous player. Romano is a more defensive player but
he's a good crosser of the ball.

Ireland – Carranza can be a bit frustrating but the fans love him,
although a lot of things don't come off for him. Maybe he
should be given the right-hand side role with Garrido on the
left. Some fans think Romano is Ivano's pal and that keeps
him in. Ivano also says Gavin Rae is the complete player, but
he's really far from it at the moment.

Grimmond – Rae has always had the ability to go all the way but
maybe doesn't have the swagger that some of the
Argentinians have. He's physically strong but doesn't always
use it. I get the feeling they were hoping he would be sold
by now. I think that Mark Robertson has the potential to fill
the position. Caballero is struggling to last a full game.

Ireland – They think he'll be right by Christmas. His shot is
fantastic and, when he cuts inside, it's hard to defend
against. It was fantastic to see him come back last season at
Parkhead. We were sitting in front of his girlfriend and the
joy on his face when he scored and gave her a wave – we felt
good for him.

Grimmond – He's still never had a proper run with Sara and he's still losing weight. Claudio, of course, was the PR dream.

Ireland – My photograph was on the back of a tabloid, wearing the blond wig. We actually met him at that time, which was fantastic.

Grimmond – My greatest memory would be after the 2–0 derby game at Tannadice. He was in the High Corner that night, pulling pints. Fans were getting autographs on their bellies to be tattooed there the next day, a lifelong memento.

Ireland – There was his first touch on his debut. People will never forget that day. He just picked the ball up. He hadn't played for months, yet there was that classy touch and the classy finish. There was the top-six finish tension too, also at Aberdeen. We got a slagging for celebrating that but everyone had achieved what they set out to do. All that hard work; we deserved it. Now we're saying that when Ivano goes, we're gonna emigrate and support his new team. It's a joke but, at the end of the day, I know of people on the supporters' bus who only stay in Dundee because of what's happening at the club. I know I couldn't move away.

Grimmond – There was a defining moment at Ibrox when Jocky was manager. There was talk of merger with United. There was still this demonstration by a small band of diehard fans, organised by the JMB, to maintain the club's independence. Nobody wanted a merger, and the club started getting better players in again. However, if we're getting a new stadium for sweeties – money from the Scottish Executive – why not?

Ireland – It makes us vulnerable, however. Peter Marr might sell and suddenly United is up for sale. It's people's lives, not just a business.

Grimmond – A merger would kill both clubs. They would lose both core supports. Dundee having two teams defies logic, but last year we were on a high all the way through. Also, everything changes with results but every time we look

ahead at the fixture list we never seem to win these 'easy'
games. They've had a number of bad injuries too.

Ireland – But there's still excitement all the time. Today it's the
China captain or Ketsbaia that's coming to Dens.

Grimmond – It's also widening the fans' horizons. They're wearing
the Argentine and Italian colours and probably seeing these
teams in an entirely different light. It's an amazing time in
our lives.

TWENTY-ONE

IVANO AND DARIO (PART ONE)

Dario Magri

I started to say to Ivano, 'This is the place . . .'

I had noticed Dario Magri, the club co-ordinator, in the pre-match warm-ups but would not have thought to interview him had I not heard a short press briefing he gave at Dens one day. He obviously knew the Bonettis intimately and had Ivano's trust. His English is excellent (he also speaks French, Spanish and a little Arabic, as well as his native Italian) and his quiet confidence was impressive.

He told me: 'I come originally from the same place as Ivano and Dario. They lived on the outskirts of Brescia, I'm from further south, closer to Lake Garda. I was born in 1958. I'm related to them through marriage – my cousin married the third Bonetti brother. My father was originally from Brescia and my mother was from Bari in the south, although she was raised in the north. I played football at school and later as an amateur in my home town. I was a bit of a donkey at school, although quite good at languages – Italian, French and Latin – and I didn't need to study much to learn them. It's also the reason I came to England, to learn the language.

'My teenage years were just at the end of the hippie period and my dream was to travel. I went round Italy and to the Greek Islands on a pushbike. But I was also playing football. Gianni Rivera, the golden boy of Italian football, was coming to the end of his career at this time. The most prominent names were Mazzola and Bonisegna the striker.

'Dario [Bonetti] was born in 1961 and Ivano in 1964. Their older brother Mario was the first of the family to break into the professional game, although I think their father played in the Brescia youth side. Mario played for Atalanta in Serie A with Guitano Scirea, who became the national captain and captain of Juventus [he died in 1991 in a car crash]. Mario was very good but had to retire through injured cruciates when he was still quite young. So then he would take his brothers to an area of the town which is very much part of the Italian tradition, the *oratorio*, where all the kids play football. It's normally an enclosed area next to the church where kids can have fun and play football in safety. It may have been a public speaking area in the old days.

'I remember English football well at this time – Bobby Charlton and George Best, who I thought was English. Scotland did not mean so much. They were thought of as a team of warriors – whenever you played them, you'd have trouble because they were physically so committed. And I remember the Italians didn't like to play against Celtic or Rangers; they were difficult teams.

'Come the age of 19, I went for military service. However, I was otherwise politically committed. At the end of the hippie period you wanted to fight for peace rather than war so I was a conscientious objector, which meant one of two things. Either you accepted "alternative" service, which I wanted to do, or you went to prison. I offered to work in hospitals but they refused and I went to prison for 13 months. It was not a nice experience but I had taken the step. The first prison was an old monastery on Lake Garda where you had freedom within the walls, but the second was the Alcatraz of Italy, an ancient castle on the sea between Rome and Naples called Gaeta – a prison for 1,000 years which was not really fit for human habitation. They closed it ten days after I came out [in September 1979]. I didn't really have a well-defined political position; maybe *lotta continua* [ongoing struggle]. I had worked in a factory and was a union representative but I didn't like the extremists. There was a bad fascist bombing at a rally in Brescia in 1974 when 30 people died. Also, in the first of the two prisons I went to, I met a young kid who was the son of a director of RAI TV, a spoiled kid who had very extreme fascist ideas. Two years later, he was the guy who bombed Bologna in 1980. Giusva Fioravanti was his name.

'Meanwhile Dario Bonetti was having a great career. He reached the Champions' League final with Roma in 1984. He also played against Dundee United that year, then, when Berlusconi took over at AC Milan, Dario was the first player he wanted to buy. He had played under Nils Liedholm at Roma and Niedholm took him to Milan. Dario, however, then fell out with a new, young coach, Arrigo Sacchi (who would become the most successful coach in the country) and went to a smaller team, Verona, which was full of talent and doing well at the time. There he met a certain Claudio Caniggia who had just come to Italy (in 1988). Dario also played for the national team and had two years at Juve under Dino Zoff, when Baggio was there.

'Claudio was called "The Bird" because he used to "fly". Everybody raved about his pace and the speed of his reactions. Maradona was at Naples at this time and any time I was with Ivano and Dario and they would meet other players, the subject of Maradona always came up. I don't remember a single player of Dario's age ever disagreeing about who the best-ever player was. He was on a different level. I asked Caniggia a lot about this time when he was in Dundee. He used to tell me that because they were also close friends, Maradona always knew when he got the ball, where Claudio was going to go. And you don't catch Caniggia once he's gone. We had a lot of interest from Argentina when Claudio was here and everyone would say that, in their history, while Maradona was considered the greatest, Claudio was next. He loved the human side of Dundee.

'Ivano started at Brescia. He was bought by Juventus but they sent him on loan for a year to the club Genoa. In 1985 he went back to Juve and played there for two and half years, winning the League. After that he went to Atalanta, made it to the semi-final of the Cup Winners' Cup, stayed there one year then went to Bologna for two years. From Bologna, he went to Sampdoria. At Juve and Bologna he played with Cabrini, the great full-back, and Scirea. One of the coaches at Juventus was Trappatoni, who he regards as the best; a complete coach and a balanced man who knew how to keep 11 champions together. There was Paolo Rossi, Platini, Boniek, and Dino Zoff was in goal. At Sampdoria, he played with Vialli, Mancini, Pagliuca and Cerezo, the Brazilian. The coach was the Yugoslavian national coach, Boskov, and they won the League and reached the final of the Champions League.

'I decided to come to London in 1979, and spoke zero English. The first job I tried for, I said "Is my name Dario" instead of "My name is Dario" and the woman probably said "Well, if *you* don't know . . ." So I studied with the help of a book, and 45 days later she gave me a job. My accent was pure Cockney by the mid-'80s and I stayed until 1991, having started a cleaning and construction company.

'I had a contract with the chairman and senior members of the BCCI Bank. I was trusted and used to look after their private properties. The bank collapsed, however, they left the country, and I was left without a penny. I was in the Caribbean when I learned the bank had closed on 5 July 1991. Because I worked for the bosses, I was offered work by a Pakistani noblewoman who was related to the Aga Khan and she suggested we set up a business in Islamabad, cleaning palatial properties. I said yes and travelled to Italy to get marble-cleaning equipment. I met Ivano and Dario and they said, "Don't go there, stay in Italy and work with us."

'So I moved in with them in Sampdoria. Their dream was to eventually get a team of their own. They had invested wisely – their main house was on Lake Garda, there's a waterfront apartment in Genoa with a boat, and a property in Sardinia – but those were early days and at first we did other things. By then I had a lot of international experience and contacts. Initially I bought classic cars for footballers and this led to showbusiness. Ivano's girlfriend at the time was a famous singer and TV presenter. One day, her manager asked me to look after some US soap stars from *Beverly Hills 90210*, who had come to Italy, where it was very successful. After three days the stars' manager wanted me to take over the European contract and I was invited back to the States. I was there when, one day, Ivano phoned me to say there was a business opportunity in the Middle East, buying and selling raw materials like aluminium. So I went to Cairo and stayed there nine months. I loved it and even bought a restaurant on the Red Sea!

'One day, Ivano called again. He had broken up with his girlfriend and was planning to play in Japan. "But before their season begins," he said, "I've been offered to play for a little club in England and I'd like you to go with me."

'There was an Italian manager named Paladini, who lived in Manchester and had worked with Bryan Robson of Middlesbrough. He said Ivano should try Grimsby. I remember we arrived in Manchester at 5 p.m. and Ivano had been sick all week. I said we should rest tonight then see the club tomorrow, but the guy said, "You're playing tonight, 7.45." We just got there in time. It was a reserve game and there were 2,000 people. We didn't know that that was not normal and that they had all come to see Ivano, but they'd heard a Serie A player was coming, and he had a wonderful game. In the Coca-Cola Cup three days later he got man of the match and after a few League games they had moved from close to the bottom to second in the First Division.

'He thought he was coming to play with a team for three or four months, to get himself fit [in 1995–96]. Coming from a fairly glamorous background, approaching Grimsby for the first time was a bit of a shock. Ivano had a lifestyle in Genoa that most could only dream of: the boat under the house, lunch in Portofino. Anyway, here we were at Blundel Park. We've laughed about it many times. They put us into a bed and breakfast opposite. The youngest waitress was about 65 and we were in a single room with Ivano in the bed and me on the floor. There was no toilet and it was a bit bigger than a cupboard. Ivano goes, "I'm a millionaire. Why the eff am I living in this dump?" But the people were brilliant, so nice.

'It got to the stage that you'd go into a pub and buy the Bonetti beer; into the pizzeria there's the Bonetti pizza . . . Bonetti garden gnomes. There was the old story about the dressing-room incident, but a young manager is either humble and glad to see a great player . . . or he's a prima donna. The team loved Ivano and, after the punching incident, they lost 5–0, 3–0. The manager was doing everything he could to get rid of Ivano and the club had no experience of such problems. Ivano wasn't even expecting to play a number of games and he got a derisory offer, so he moved on. One of the teams we had beaten was Tranmere, where Ivano had scored and played a blinder. John Aldridge was really impressed and invited him to play there next, and Ivano became very friendly with Pat Nevin. After seven games, both players were suddenly dropped – and nobody knew why, because Pat is also such a gentleman, but that was the end of Ivano playing in England.

'Ivano was not the first Italian to play in England in this (modern) period, but he was the first to score. When Tranmere finished, I went back to Egypt [in 1997]. I was running the restaurant but it was to close for three months and Ivano was back in Italy, so I thought I'd go back to London. I picked up the *South London Press* and saw that Atillio Lombardo was coming to Crystal Palace as a player. So that was ideal. He was a friend and I went along to Selhurst Park and offered to be his interpreter. The club wanted me to fill in an application form so I called Lombardo and asked him to put me in his contract, which he was happy to do. He had been at Sampdoria with Ivano then moved to Juventus. So I started off as an interpreter but eventually became what I am in Dundee, looking after the foreign players. I had a good relationship with the new chairman, Mark Alberg, who unfortunately lost everything. And I suggested Atillio as player/manager. Then I suggested Ivano and he came over and played well, but he only got two games, against Arsenal and Sheffield Wednesday [in late 1997], because the club did not want to give him a longer contract – although Genoa did.

'Ivano had seen the potential of First Division clubs in England. He'd say, "People here are mad about football, yet the clubs are run very unprofessionally: diet, training methods, etc. I can only imagine what these players could do if they put these things right." We came close to buying Grimsby (Ivano would have been player/chairman) and we tried Hull City but that didn't work either. Ivano asked me to keep an eye out for any similar opportunities.

'Eventually, one day in October 1999, this guy Borko calls me, whom I knew because I had helped take one of his players to Palace from Aston Villa. I linked up with him and he said he had a friend in Dundee who needed players and did I have anyone. I said I had a midfielder who could go on trial. So I came to Dundee (with Patrizio Billio who Steve Coppell was not giving a chance at Palace) and Walter Del Rio. They played a reserve game at Tannadice and Walter was turned down, although he had a blinding game. Jocky Scott thought he was no better than what he had and I was really shocked. Anyway, he took on Billio and I came here a few times, saw what the town was like and I tried to see into the future as far as Ivano and myself were concerned. I started to say to him, "Look, this is the place. The chairman is very open-minded and wants to go places. I don't think he's happy the way things are run." I brought Ivano over for one of the derbys and he spoke to Jim Connor and Peter Marr and we made friends.

'Ivano was not looking at money. He wanted a club where he could implement the ideas that he and Dario had learned in 20 years of Italian football and prove a point that, without much money, you can still succeed. We started with no money and took in a lot of glamorous players – even Zurab cost only a small fee.

'Training follows scientific logic. It is not casual but done in such a way that, come Saturday, you are at your peak. You never do hard work on a Friday. Monday is one programme, Tuesday and Wednesday you take the fuel in, build the muscles, hard work. Thursday is a day off the park, relaxing, massage, foot tennis and Friday is tactical work and making sure your body is ready for the game. The tactical plan means that the youngsters can come into the scheme of things easily. There is a lot of emphasis on weight and diet, and physiotherapy to us is paramount. Giovanni Grassi is the physio and Claudio Bozzini the goalkeeping coach.

'I also like to think that I have introduced the role of team support manager from Italy to the UK – he makes sure problems don't spread and tries not to make a fuss [by going to the manager]. Also I try to make sure that the efforts of the whole club are co-ordinated towards the efforts of the first team. I'm not trying to overstate my own role. The assets of a club are the players, so we must look after their interests. The best club in the world for all this stuff is AC Milan. Helping them with cars, housing, gas and electricity, day-to-day problems; giving them support. Paul Marr has been a great help in this area.

'It was a lot easier for us to appreciate Dundee, thanks to Grimsby. When we went there, everyone said, "It's the armpit of England. It's a dump." Yet we had a wonderful experience there. We even liked the place. So we realised that if you adopt the right mental attitude towards the place you go to, you will see the nice side, not only the bad side. Of course Dundee has a bad side, but when we approached the place we approached it positively. We were looking for the good things in Dundee and we found them immediately. The people first of all. They were very friendly. I have lived half of my life in London and you never know who your next-door neighbour is. In Dundee you can make friends easily. Also, several parts of the town and surrounding areas are absolutely beautiful. You lead a quiet life, but you can focus on your job. I have gone to the west coast and the islands, I like to visit castles and lochs. The boys travel mainly to cities but some have been up north and there is a lot to see.

'We are still not a wealthy club, although the Marrs have done all they can possibly do. But no one can deny that we produce good football. I heard someone say "take away the goalposts and we are the most entertaining team in the SPL". Now we are trying to step up for this year, possibly get a UEFA spot. That would be ideal.

'We haven't finished with good news for Dundee. This year I think the news will be very good. We have very valid additions and once we get those in, we will aim higher. Our squad has been reduced to cut costs but Ivano's dream is to have 22 players, two for each position. Eleven starters, five on the bench who are just as good, and five young, possibly local, kids. We're doing better in this area.

'Peter Marr realises exactly what we want to do and appreciates it will not happen overnight. To grow a strong tree takes time. And we're also working on a non-existent budget, but we are working together and soon we will be in a better position. Maybe we'll get outside investors or companies who would give long-term support. Many clubs around the UK are doing this now. And Dario and Ivano are so committed to Dundee, they are already investing themselves. I think any foreigner thinks of going home in the long run, but that long run could be many years. We can't do something really good in Dundee unless we stay here a long time so we are not looking at going anywhere.'

TWENTY-TWO

IVANO AND DARIO (PART TWO)

BONETTI'S BLUES

It's a beautiful August day in Dundee and, from memory, the Bonetti brothers have not seen too many of them since they arrived just over a year ago. Dens Park is gleaming in the sunshine and even Caird Park Stadium, where the players are training, looks like a quality facility (which it is, if not in the Rangers class). I resist telling anyone that this is the crucible of my own, brief athletic and footballing career.

Ivano looks a lot like his older brother Dario but the coach is a large and imposing man as befits a former Italian international *libero,* while Ivano cuts a more tailored figure, who today prowls around the perimeter whilst his brother brings his experience to bear on the team's back four which struggled at the weekend. The goalkeepers work separately and Ivano watches the action, intervening if a player does not appear to be taking things in satisfactorily. The instruction is multi-lingual, Italian giving way to English and Spanish, but the players noticeably work harmoniously as a group, including the two gifted Georgians, Nemsadze and Zurab, who are having to pick up a bit of everything as they go along. I think how young the squad looks (Jamie Langfield, Beto Carranza, Stephen Milne and Juan Sara) and how much responsibility is put upon their young shoulders by management, fans and the press.

Ivano also looks more youthful in close proximity than he does in the dugout or on TV. Perhaps the office of manager confers age and wisdom. In spite of a prior club appointment he is slightly surprised to see me but the warmth of his personality comes across immediately and he offers a brief chat whilst continuing to maintain a watchful eye on the training. My jacket is duly hung over a steeplechase hurdle and away we go.

Born in the northern Italian town of Brescia, an industrial centre with a population of around 300,000, Ivano was one of four children, three boys and a girl.

'My father played for Brescia but he was 24 years old when the war intervened and there were more important things to think about. Dario then went to Brescia as a teenager but I had no particular desire to be a professional footballer at first. I was only 16 and still thinking about school and everything when I played my first games for the club. Gianni Rivera was a top Italian player I remember from this time and he was coming to the end of his career.

'Dario had a great playing career: Roma (he was in the team which played Dundee United in the European Cup); Sampdoria; Milan (with Franco Baresi, although the great Dutch players had not yet arrived); and Verona, where he played with Claudio Caniggia. I also met Claudio around this time; he was in Italy for a number of years.

'I, too, played with some fine players: Platini at Juve was probably the best (although Diego Maradona was, of course, the *very* best player when he played in Italy), and Vialli and others at Sampdoria. We won the Italian League and got to the Champions League final, which was played at Wembley that year. We lost to Barcelona. I tended to play on the left-wing or left-midfield. And there were great coaches like Trappatoni and Eriksson.

'When I reached the age of 30, I felt I wanted to spread my wings a little, to go and play in another country to learn something of the game there, the culture and language. I was particularly keen to try England. Football had been my life and I had learned a lot about the game so it was natural to want to try management.

'I was introduced to Peter Marr by my friend Dario Magri, and spent a lot of time talking to him about my management ideas and my contacts, and I thought Dundee had good potential. Of course, you need money but I have some outstanding young players – three great strikers, Zurab, and now Walter Del Rio is coming through and the squad value must be £20 million. I am already thinking about next season, buying and selling new players.'

Ivano has been a breath of fresh air in the Scottish game – frank, outspoken, calling spades shovels – and fan Robin Grimmond's observation (in chapter 20) that this at one point gave the press and referees open season on him and his players is not entirely invalid.

'I am still trying to get the squad up to 22. We know we didn't get the results we should have last season and we must keep working. The main thing is, I have chosen the right club with ambition to go forwards. Nothing in football is impossible. I know I have my own attitudes which may be different from some of those in Scotland but I have only started here.'

Refereeing is a real bugbear. He has been sent off as a player and cautioned, along with his brother, as a manager. There was one classic moment of frustration at Kilmarnock when he casually hoofed some guy up in the air and walked off to be substituted in the same movement before the referee could react. So no one is suggesting he is an angel, but his team has faced a lot of inconsistency from the men in black.

'They should take responsibility,' he says, 'just like I ask players to. Maybe a stand official would make a difference. I just don't like the fact they can't be criticised.'

Ivano is also at ease with the foreign/Scottish player ratio. 'My Scottish players learn from people like Nemsadze and Caballero and will improve as the squad improves. We are laying the foundations for something good in future years.'

Ivano displays confidence and, this being August, a degree of forward thinking. Indeed, earlier in the week Peter Marr had announced his intention to offer Ivano and Dario a two-year extension to their contracts and my distinct impression was that they were going to carry on. There was also talk of marriage and a home in Dundee for the manager.

But, surprise surprise, he has nothing really to 'reveal'. That's because the revelation is his team – Bonetti's Blues – who have come to the club knowing little of its history, perhaps pleased that it has some, and trustful of the two brothers whose playing careers speak for themselves and who, they believe, will improve them not only as individual players, but also as team players and will transfer them – if and when the time comes – sensibly.

There is no secret. The team needs a sound defence, a creative midfield and goalscoring forwards. Everyone seeks entry into European football. Instead of trawling the lower divisions as its predecessors have always done, the modern club trawls the world, fishers of men and, luckily for the Dundee fans, forward-thinking business management has come together with forward-thinking coaching. The synergy has put a team on the park which still struggles to win, but always entertains in the best possible way – through sheer footballing skill.

I think what we are seeing at Dens Park is another example of an ambitious club working *in partnership* with a manager, rather than *employing* him. Graeme Souness was shaping up for a similar role at Rangers: an individual who had made a personal fortune as a player, using his contacts to offer high-profile player continuity and gradually taking a stake in the club – and Ivano continues to demonstrate the same ability to bring amazing signings out of the hat. Ryan Ireland's comments (in chapter 20) demonstrate that the fans had wind of something special coming up again but the press retained a cynical 'seeing is believing' stance until an amazing week in mid-October 2001.

Following a string of disappointing performances, Peter Marr announces that the club has made its biggest commercial signing since Claudio Caniggia almost exactly one year previously. The Chinese national captain and central defender Fan Zhiyi (31), said by many to be the best player yet produced by that amazing, massive country, has signed a two-year contract from Crystal Palace. The fee, a reported £350,000, was substantially less than his £2 million estimated value, because Dundee had agreed to meet his high salary requirements and the deal was completed by Dario Magri in China. Indeed, it is later reported that Dundee will play in the Orient against the national side as part of China's World Cup preparations and the club's website is apparently immediately inundated with hits from China.

Fan had led his country to the 2002 World Cup finals (to be played in Japan and Korea) and was reported as saying that the regular games which he was promised by Dundee would be crucial to his build-up. It was hoped, as with Claudio, that such a signing would open up new, worldwide commercial opportunities. There is, for example, said to be a 60-foot poster of the player alongside one of David Beckham in Beijing. Ivano is not yet finished though, for within 48 hours, the Georgian international and former Newcastle United midfielder Temuri Ketsbaia has joined the Dark Blues from Wolves. Again there is talk of the positive value of the Georgian connection (and of high salaries) but Ketsbaia is upbeat: 'Giorgi has told me about the club and their ambition. There are international players coming here and they're trying to do something special.'

Right on cue, Brescia's Polish international midfielder Marek Kozminski is said to be expected to sign at the end of the month while ex-Serie A wing-back Massimo Begehetto is suggested as a possible replacement for the injured Marrocco. This news also coincides with a financial report that the outlook will be bleak for Scottish clubs if the Old Firm defect to the English Premiership. Each of the minnows is said to derive a fifth of their annual turnover from the four home games against Celtic and Rangers. Dundee have apparently shown pre-tax losses of £760,000 on season 1999–2000 (i.e. pre-Ivano) with attendances around 57 per cent of capacity. Figures for the next two seasons will be most interesting and the whole Old Firm/Premiership/Atlantic League or whatever-the-future-holds issue must also have implications for Dundee.

Would Scottish clubs flounder if the Old Firm defect, or would an increased chance of European qualification spur teams on and retain, or even increase, the number of fans? Would one city of Dundee club stand a better chance in a European league?

Football is a simple game, but different people will always have different ideas and different levels of ambition: some Dundee fans think things will go no farther and eventually peter out (no pun intended); some think a cup is a possibility; some think yet higher, while others grumble about where the money is coming from. What principally pleases me is that the ordinary supporter is not wrong in his beliefs – that the game can be exquisite and rewarding if properly handled – and, perhaps most important of all, that their club is back on the national, and even the international, map. For the foreseeable future, it will be watched closely, not only by Dundee supporters but also by the wider footballing community and, indeed, the wider world as a progressive organisation, something which reflects not only upon those fans, but the city as a whole. One former player politely declined an interview saying, 'I mean, Ivano Bonetti's only been here a couple of seasons,' but I think this misses the point. The important point for Dundee Football Club and its fans is *how he got here,* how *they, the fans,* got here and where we all go *from* here.

I would like to think that the youngsters who are currently inspired by the efforts of Bonetti's Blues will be happy to carry on the traditions of Dundee Football Club in years to come.